DATE DUE

The Morals of Markets

The Morals of Markets

An Ethical Exploration

H. B. Acton

Longman
in association with
The Institute of Economic Affairs

LONGMAN GROUP LIMITED
London
*Associated companies, branches and representatives
throughout the world*

© Longman Group Limited 1971

First published 1971

ISBN 0 582 50028 1

Printed in Great Britain by The Camelot Press Ltd,
London and Southampton

Contents

Foreword

The IEA is to be congratulated for having sponsored this essay by Professor Acton. He is a distinguished philosopher with a profound interest in moral philosophy.

In this essay he applies his acute mind to the morality of the market system; the system under which goods and services are produced and distributed competitively for profit at the risk of the producers and distributors.

This system has brought about unprecedented economic growth and continues so to do. It is the risk taken by venturers and their backers that has led to the introduction of products that in course of time come to be taken for granted. Examples are the supply of electricity, the pneumatic tyre and the internal combustion engine. It is inconceivable that any of these things could have been ordered by some consumer's committee. In fact they all had to fight their way to recognition. The future is unknown and unprovable. New ideas are of necessity, risky. Novelty generally seems dotty and is always ridiculed by vested interests which stand for the past, or at best the present.

Nor is it true to say that in modern times risk-taking and the provision of risk capital has ceased. It takes place on an enormous scale, for example, in the search for North Sea gas. One does not hear much of the failures and losses. Only the successes are publicised and popularised. Risk-taking has also been and continues to be a powerful instrument of human freedom. A producer of goods or services can at his own choice exchange the fruit of his labours for an enormous range of products coming from areas as remote as China or Peru and the Arctic or Antarctic or the Tropics. Moreover through the price mechanism everyone can establish his own personal priorities of wants and satisfactions and call on the goods and services of others according to his own choice. The consumer must choose what he will buy and what he will do without. This responsibility of choosing is an essential element in all freedom.

Nevertheless this system has been under attack for very many years. It has been held responsible by one writer or another for every ill from which man can suffer, not excluding human folly or wickedness. One line of attack, and an insidious one, has been to throw doubt on the morality of working in hope of a profit. This speculative and uncertain form of remuneration has been rated lower in the moral scale than the contractual and certain remuneration in wages, salaries or professional fees. Indeed it is often declared to be absolutely immoral because it is thought to be based on pure selfishness which is often contrasted with the high-mindedness of public and professional motivation.

Having lived myself in all three worlds I can only say that this superior morality has not been noticeable to me. But this propaganda has had its effect not only upon critics of the system, but upon businessmen themselves. It has lowered their morale. They have become all too prone to succumb to appeals based on the so-called 'public interest', which usually means no more than a politician's momentary idea of what ought to be done. Profit stems mainly from the economical use of any given quantity of resources. This is the primary economic need of any community, and anyone who serves it is a public benefactor and should not be put off by abuse of private interest. The propaganda has also certainly influenced the university graduate in his choice of career.

It is this question of morality that Professor Acton discusses and analyses with stimulating freshness and clarity. His examination leads him to the conclusion that anti-market propaganda for all its high moral tone is full of contradictions and unanalysed assumptions which he elucidates.

This essay is not within the usual range of reading of many business men. But it should be recommended reading for all. It will bring them a clearer idea of what they are really doing and a clear conscience in doing it.

TANGLEY

Preface

I am very grateful for help (not always taken) and advice (from which I have greatly profited) from Arthur Seldon, Ralph Harris, George Schwartz, John B. Wood and Hamish Gray. I should also like to express my admiration for Mr Seldon's patience in allowing me to have second thoughts and rather long delayed ones.

H. B. Acton

March, 1970

I. The Theme of the Essay

The unpopularity of free markets

The purpose of this essay is to examine, from the point of view of morality, the merits, for merits there assuredly are, and the defects, for there are defects in all human institutions, of the system under which goods are produced for sale at a profit in free markets. This system stands morally condemned by a large part of our population. In schools and universities the *laissez-faire*[1] philosophy is attacked by many historians who describe and expose the harshnesses of its initial operation, and by almost all social scientists, who assume that it is outmoded and tell their students so. Competition is regarded as a form of strife, markets as 'jungles', and 'the profit motive' as disreputable. Collectivists, of course, by the very nature of their creed, wish to control and limit the workings of markets, but non-collectivists, too, have been influenced by their opponents and often believe that it would be unchristian to oppose the imposition of more control by governments over economic activities. Indeed, it is assumed that since for a long time now the tendency has been for governments to try to control the economy and to limit the extent of free markets, there is some-

[1] The phrase *laissez-faire, laissez-passer* was used in the eighteenth century by a member of the group of French political economists known as Physiocrats. The Physiocrats criticised the so-called Mercantilist System under which the government controlled the manufacture and pricing of goods, the location of industries, and the movement of trade, with the aim of securing a favourable balance of trade for the country. The Physiocrats, as their name indicates—the Greek word *physis* means 'nature'—favoured a more spontaneous, natural and less artificial industrial and commercial system. Hence, *laissez-faire* meant 'let people produce' or 'let them get on with the job', and *laissez-passer* meant 'let people move around as they please'. Adam Smith was influenced by some of the arguments of the Physiocrats when, in *The Wealth of Nations* (1776), he argued that national prosperity is more likely to result from allowing goods to be freely produced and exchanged than from controlling production and exchange by governmental means. Carlyle used the expression *laissez-faire* in *Chartism* (1839), in a pejorative sense, implying that a government that does not intervene in economic affairs is failing in its duty. A striking feature of our own times is the revival of Mercantilism and a corresponding diminution of regard for economic freedom. In these circumstances *laissez-faire* tends to be an abusive term. It should be noticed that Adam Smith and his followers did not say that governments should never on any account intervene in industry and commerce.

thing quixotic, reactionary, or positively wicked in the idea of trying to move in the opposite direction.

Yet it is just when a social outlook has hardened into a dogma that it is most necessary to examine it in the light of possible alternatives. The time when 'we are all socialists' is the very time to reconsider the morality of the free market, which may be more often traduced than understood. If free markets are bad, the reasons why they are bad should be clearly stated. If they are not wholly bad, then the prevailing outlook needs to be modified. Past theories and policies and the lack of them have built up interests and influences whose presuppositions should not remain unquestioned.

Markets: a preliminary analysis

In the non-technical sense of the word, markets are *places* where goods are bought and sold. In small market towns farmers still bring produce to these places and wait for customers to come and buy. As the goods are on display, the buyers will look for the best goods at the cheapest prices. No one will knowingly pay sixpence a pound for potatoes when he can buy equally good ones somewhere else in the market for threepence a pound, and so the price of potatoes of similar quality tends to be the same, and a market price is established. In rather more sophisticated markets the goods have been bought from the producers by merchants who in their turn perhaps sell them to other merchants or to shopkeepers. In such markets both sellers and buyers are generally very well informed about what the producers have for sale and what demand there is from consumers. The goods are finely graded according to quality, and a market price for each grade is established as buyers ascertain what is on offer and how much of it there is.

When all or most of the products consumed in a society are distributed in this way, the society is said to have a market or exchange economy. In a market economy goods are produced with a view to their being sold through wholesalers and retailers. It is expected that the merchants who buy the products will give prices in accordance with the quality of the goods and in accordance with what they expect or hope to get from retailers or consumers. Merchants can choose between different producers, retailers can choose between the goods offered by different wholesalers, and consumers can go to the shop which seems to them to offer the goods they most want at prices they are willing to pay. When the system is competitive[1] merchants can buy from this producer or that, producers can sell to this merchant or that, and ultimately the consumer with money to spend can choose which shop to go to. Hence the producer tries to produce goods which merchants will want to buy, merchants will try to buy goods which retailers feel sure they can sell, and consumers will go to the shop which they think offers them what they most want to have at prices which they think lowest for the quality they want.

A further feature of the market economy that must be mentioned at this stage is that the competing producers and competing merchants and shopkeepers are not, in general, individuals (although some of them are), but firms which employ individuals to work for them in exchange for wages or salaries. In a completely free market individuals could, subject to their contracts of employment, leave one firm and work for another which offered better terms, and employing firms could, again subject to their contracts with their employees, dismiss employees whose work they do not find satisfactory. The system is quite compatible with fairly long-term contracts between firms and employees, and with complex contracts between them on holidays, conditions of work and pensions.

Producing and merchanting firms are not only producers and merchants but also consumers of goods produced and distributed by other producers and merchants. For example, a producer of motor-cars is a consumer of steel which he buys (perhaps through a merchant) from a steel producer, and a merchant consumes in the course of his business at the very least notepaper and office furniture. Ultimate consumers, apart from children and retired and chronically sick people, are also producers, but of course each consumer consumes a much wider range of goods than as a wage earner he has helped to produce. It is important to notice that a very large proportion of the people who are active in the market economy are employed for wages or salaries by the firms which compete in producing and distributing the goods consumed in it. Within

[1] Monopoly is discussed below, pp. 55–7.

a market economy the most widely shared economic experiences
are those involved in selling one's labour and in buying consumer goods. The more sophisticated economic experiences are
confined to a relatively small class.

Some presuppositions of this analysis

The highly simplified sort of organisation so far described presupposes at least five sets of circumstances. Firstly it assumes a
division of labour and normally the use of money. In it the
producer of one sort of product sells it for money which he uses
in buying products which he does not make himself.

Secondly it presupposes that those taking part in the transactions involved are all trying to do as well as they can for
themselves and for their families. Producers and merchants
want to get the best possible price for what they sell, and
merchants and consumers do not want to pay more than they
have to. In general, if someone pays too high a price or agrees
to sell at too low a price, this will be through inadvertence,
laziness, ignorance or a benevolent whim. If a man loses
money for these reasons, he is not expected to blame anyone
but himself, and if he does such things too often he will drop out
of the system. Fraud and deliberate deception are, as we shall
see, defined in the legal rules under which the system operates,
and when detected they lead to punishments of various kinds.
Dishonesty that cannot readily be dealt with in courts of law,
such as denying or altering verbal agreements, is generally
left to be countered by such methods as refusing to have further
dealings with the perpetrator, as when consumers withdraw
their custom. The various parties are expected to be honest,
and it is hoped that if they are tempted to be dishonest they will
be prevented by fear of losing business, if not by the strength of
their moral principles.

Thirdly, although it is possible for goods to be exchanged
without the existence of law and government,[1] continuous
market operations require there to be laws against fraud and
violence, and governments to enforce the laws. It can hardly
be expected that no one will ever try to bully or to cheat in

---

[1] Indeed, it has been surmised that the earliest markets were held between the
members of different hostile tribes who each needed what the other had and rather
stealthily made the exchange in the wilderness.

order to get what he wants. Even if all the parties were trying to be just, they could differ about the meaning of the agreements they have made and be obstinate in defence of their own point of view. The rules must be stated, interpreted and enforced, and for this framework of laws some sort of government is required. It need not be the state,[1] but where states exist the creation of this legal framework is a function they are universally expected to perform or to ensure that others perform. Just as some games require referees or umpires, so market economies require courts and police. Like football players, the participants are in general expected to institute and pursue their own strategies, but in both cases there are limits upon what they are allowed to do to one another.

Fourthly, it is generally agreed that private property is essential to the effective operation of the market economy. The idea has been that in buying and selling the seller receives money for what was originally his property and that the buyer, in passing over the money, gets in return the ownership of the goods. The market economy is thus generally regarded as an economy in which private enterprise predominates. Although markets may exist in socialist societies when quasi-independent producing bodies are allowed to compete for orders from the government or when producing organisations compete in selling goods to the governmental retail stores,[2] our discussion is not concerned with this socialist sort of market.[3]

A final presupposition of a market economy is that no market or series of markets comprises the whole of a society. There have been societies without markets, and when markets have eventually been set up in them some of the earlier methods of distributing goods have continued, as when clothes are made within the family, but the needles and thread for making them are purchased from elsewhere. When I said above that someone who persistently sells too cheaply or buys too dear 'will drop out of the system', I did not mean that he will vanish

[1] The Stock Exchange and certain commodity markets draw up their own rules.
[2] See Margaret Miller and others, *Communist Economy under Change: Studies in the theory and practice of markets and competition in Russia, Poland and Yugoslavia*, London, Institute of Economic Affairs, 1963.
[3] Market *analysis* may also be appropriate to wholly planned economies without competition to determine whether resources in the economy are being effectively allocated. Professor Bela Csikos-Nagy, *Pricing in Hungary*, London, Institute of Economic Affairs, 1968.

5

from society altogether. In all societies with market economies some arrangements are made to help casualties of the system. Again, it is not merely the case that some sorts of thing that might be bought and sold are not, but also that some sorts of thing ought not to be for sale at all. There is not or ought not to be a market price for everything. It would be quite easy to buy and sell parliamentary votes, but it is illegal as well as morally wrong to do so.[1] Again, a doctor or a shopkeeper may give his help in exchange for money, but a parent does not expect payment for the help he gives to his young children, or grown-up children for the help they give their parents, or a friend for the help he gives his friend. Loyalty and love, as distinct from services or cupboard-love, are not in the market.

In market transactions all the parties are trying to make the best bargain they can. The whole mechanism presupposes that this is what they are doing. What they do with their rewards is for them to decide. Those who do well may, often do, give some to people in need, to charities or causes, social, religious or political, that they value. The market is not the place for generosity or self-sacrifice. Someone who accepts less than the market price or pays more is either under a misapprehension or else is giving something to people who do not expect to receive gifts, though no doubt they are very glad to have them. To be an unsuccessful business man is a stupid and inappropriate way of being generous. But although the market is not the place for directly exercising love and generosity, it is not the place for hatred or for treachery either.

In this section I have tried to give a brief preliminary account of competitive markets in order to prepare the way for discussion of the moral problems involved. Even at this early point of our argument, however, critics may object that the account I have given is unrealistic or irrelevant in the present era of large-scale firms and monopolies. Later in the essay I have suggested that large economic organisations which think themselves free from competition are nevertheless subject to its influence (pp. 34–7 and 55–7 below), and I have criticised the view that increasing monopoly and state control are inevitable

---

[1] Of course, politicians endeavour to get votes, in exchange for policy promises, but this is different from paying individuals for votes, which is wrong for many reasons of which we may mention two. Buying individual votes would favour richer candidates or parties. Further, it would turn voting into a matter of individual gain, whereas the system of voting requires voters to consider the general interest.

(p. 86 below). The tendency towards size and monopoly should not be exaggerated. Although the numbers of people employed in manufacturing firms with more than 10,000 workers have increased very considerably over the last thirty years, and although the proportion of the total output for which these firms are responsible has increased even more, a large proportion of employees (36 per cent) and of the net output (32 per cent) is associated with firms employing fewer than 500 workers.[1] Furthermore, the proportion of large-scale to smaller-scale firms varies from industry to industry, and even in industries where a few large firms predominate, these generally compete with one another.[2] The tendency towards greater concentration of firms, furthermore, is in part a result of public policies which could be changed.

It may be objected that there is a steady trend towards larger and larger firms and towards nationalisation and state control. But if trends are to be accepted as pointers to an inevitable future, discussion about what policies we *ought* to adopt, or about what we should *try* to do, loses point, and nothing remains except to follow the fashion. Although it is true that human beings have sometimes behaved like lemmings, I take the view that they can, by altering their views about what is desirable, change trends and even reverse them. To deny this would be to deny that the criticisms of *laissez-faire* and the preference for collectivism that developed towards the end of the last century have had anything to do with the collectivist tendencies that have shown themselves since. Of course people are apt to fall in with fashion, especially in their early years, but they can also criticise and make it. Fashions in clothes change more easily than fashions in ideas. In a way, there is something absurd in the very notion of fashions in ideas, for if ideas are merely accepted as the shops supply them, they cease to be thoughts and turn into habits. The ideas of a society in which 'trendy' is a term of praise, need a lot of shaking up.

General criticisms of the market economy

The shopkeepers and merchants who occupy such a central

[1] Census of Production 1958, Summary Table 12, and A. Armstrong and H. Silberston, 'Size of Plant, Size of Enterprise and Concentration in British Manufacturing Industry, 1935–58', *Journal of the Royal Statistical Society*, Series A, 1965.
[2] R. Evely and I. M. D. Little, *Concentration in British Industry* (Cambridge University Press, 1960).

position in the market economy have been scorned, criticised and condemned from the earliest times. Plato, who explained how markets depend upon the division of labour and the invention of money, says in the *Republic* that in well-ordered communities shopkeepers are 'generally men not strong enough to be of use in any other occupation' and are even inferior to merchants who do at least brave the dangers of going into foreign countries. Hence he placed traders of all kinds in the third and lowest class of his ideal republic, the class of those who were governed by their desires and were consequently unfit to take part in government. Aristotle, in his *Politics*, argued that it is somehow 'unnatural' and therefore bad to produce goods with the primary aim of selling them at a profit, since the purpose of production is to satisfy needs rather than to accumulate money. St Thomas Aquinas carried on the Aristotelian tradition in this as in other respects, and although he acknowledged that trading need not be 'sinful or contrary to virtue', he ruled that priests should not take part in trade since in so doing they would be diverted from spiritual things.

With the growth of economic science in the eighteenth century a rather more favourable view was taken of profits and of traders, and the classical economists, although sometimes very critical of them, argued that their activities were essential for a free and wealthy society. Thus Adam Smith in *The Wealth of Nations* (Book 2, chapter 5) wrote: 'The prejudices of some political writers against shopkeepers and tradesmen are altogether without foundation. So far is it from being necessary either to tax them or restrict their numbers that they can never be multiplied so as to hurt the public, though they may so as to hurt one another.' But this qualified approval turned out to be only a brief interlude in the continuing chorus of disapprobation. The collectivist movements of the nineteenth and twentieth centuries condemned the whole system of private competitive enterprise, claiming that it was bound to result in monopoly, injustice, widespread poverty, and eventual revolution. Influential writers of the Victorian period such as Carlyle and Ruskin criticised the system on moral grounds, and in more recent times J. A. Hobson and R. H. Tawney have revived and elaborated their arguments in order to recommend a form of socialism based on moral considerations.

Lord Robbins, in *The Theory of Economic Policy in English Classical Political Economy* (Macmillan, 1952), sets out to defend some of the classical economists from the charge of being 'very malignant creatures indeed', and in pursuing this object he emphasises those particulars in which they departed from what complete *laissez-faire* would have required. Anyone who today defends the competitive market economy is liable to be accused of favouring selfishness and inhumanity. The weary Victorian children sleeping at their machines, and the women dragging coal trucks underground are evoked to confuse and confound him.

Our present discussion is not concerned with the grandeurs and miseries of early nineteenth-century capitalism, for our questions are moral rather than historical. What we have first to consider are the grounds on which the free market economy is morally condemned. A preliminary view of them suggests the following main lines of criticism. In the first place there is the argument that the market economy, depending as it does on the 'profit motive', encourages selfishness and avarice and, indeed, exalts these vices to the rank of virtues. Then there is the argument that the competitive element in the market economy is a deplorable source of strife which should be replaced by cooperation and public service. Another criticism of the market economy is that competition inevitably leads to monopoly and so to tyranny—that what begins in freedom ends in bondage. Still another criticism is that in the workings of the market economy the purpose of production, which is the satisfaction of needs, is lost sight of, so that each individual, the capitalist or enterpriser as well as the worker, is in the grip of an impersonally operating system which takes no account of justice or morality because it is incapable of taking account of anything. Finally, the competitive market economy is contrasted with the socialistically planned economy to the detriment of the former: the competitive market economy is held to be chaotic and unjust by comparison with economies planned on socialist lines.[1]

[1] In *The Principles of Economic Planning* (Allen & Unwin, 1949) Sir William Arthur Lewis objects to what he calls the *laissez-faire* system, (1) that within it income is not fairly distributed, but is distributed in accordance with the scarcity of the resources the individuals possess, (2) that it gives no protection to employees, (3) that it is unstable, (4) that it cannot keep control of foreign trade, and (5) that it cannot cope with major change without being 'too slow and cruel' (pp. 12–14). (3) and (4) are outside the scope of this essay.

II. The Profit Motive

The immoderacy of profit

In this chapter we shall discuss the moral objection to the competitive market economy that, in depending upon the so-called 'profit motive', it encourages avarice and selfishness. This charge is complex, and we shall have to consider in turn various features of it.

One of the earliest criticisms of the market economy was put forward by Aristotle. He argued that when goods are produced for sale at a profit their use in satisfying needs is easily lost sight of and is replaced by the desire to accumulate as much money as possible. His idea was that whereas there is a limit or term to the satisfaction of needs, money can be accumulated *ad infinitum*. Hence the man who enters industry or trade in order to make money is led on by a desire that is by its very nature insatiable. The trader or money-maker introduces something inordinate and unnatural into society, and diverts attention from the satisfaction of satiable needs to the insatiable search for a limitless fortune.

It should be pointed out that any force this argument has applies not only to competitive markets but to any economy in which money is used. It is money values that can be conceived as being added to indefinitely, and these could be the gross national product of a socialist economy as well as the profits made in a competitive market economy. The contrast is really between the series of natural numbers on the one hand and satisfactions to which no numerical values in the sense of prices can be given on the other. The fact is that numbers can incite men to useless or harmful activity in any society that has a superstitious reverence for them. Profits themselves, of course, tend to be limited by competition between firms in a competitive market economy, so that any desire for the infinite is kept in check by the levelling processes of the market, so long as entry into it is free. In any case, perhaps Keynes was right when he said that 'it is better that a man should tyrannise over his bank balance than over his fellow men'.[1]

The 'Mammon Gospel'

Thomas Carlyle's *Past and Present* (1843) contains much of the rhetoric that has since been used in moral criticisms of the competitive market economy. Certain phrases in it, such as 'cash nexus'[2] and 'captains of industry' have continued in use. Carlyle's device of contrasting the socially and ecclesiastically controlled medieval economic arrangements with the individualism of nineteenth-century capitalism has been copied since, notably by R. H. Tawney in *Religion and the Rise of Capitalism* (1926). Ruskin was influenced by it when he wrote his moral condemnation of the market economy in *Unto this Last* (1862). Friedrich Engels reviewed *Past and Present* when it first came out, and incorporated something of what he had learnt from it in an essay, *Outlines of a Critique of Political Economy* (1844), from which much of the Marxist doctrine takes its origin. A paragraph from *Past and Present* (quoted by Engels in his review of it) may serve as our starting point:

True, it must be owned, we for the present, with our Mammon-Gospel, have come to strange conclusions. We call it a Society; and go about professing the totalest separation, isolation. Our life is not a mutual helpfulness; but rather, cloaked under due laws-of-war, named 'fair competition' and so forth, it is a mutual hostility. We have profoundly forgotten everywhere that *Cash-payment* is not the sole relation of human beings; we think nothing doubting, that *it* absolves and liquidates all engagements of man. 'My starving workers?' answers the rich Mill-owner: 'Did I not hire them fairly in the market? Did I not pay them, to the last sixpence, the sum covenanted for? What have I to do with them more?'—Verily Mammon-worship is a melancholy creed. When Cain for his own behoof had killed Abel, and was questioned, 'Where is thy brother?' he too made answer, 'Am I my brother's keeper?' Did I not pay my brother *his* wages, the thing he had merited from me? (First edition, pp. 198–9.)

In setting out, in chapter 1 of *Religion and the Rise of Capitalism*, the historical theme he proposes to investigate, Tawney contrasts 'the conception of society as a community of unequal classes with varying functions, organised for a common end', with 'that which regards itself as a mechanism adjusting itself

[1] J. M. Keynes, *The General Theory of Employment* (Macmillan, 1960 edn.), p. 374.
[2] Carlyle wrote of 'Cash payment the sole nexus' in *Chartism* (1839). *Critical and Miscellaneous Essays* V (1869), p. 383.

through the play of economic motives to the supply of economic needs'; he also contrasts 'the idea that a man must not take advantage of his neighbour's necessity' with 'the doctrine that "man's self-love is God's providence" ', and 'the view of economic activity which regarded it as one among other kinds of moral conduct' with 'the view of it as dependent upon impersonal and almost automatic forces'.[1]

Both Carlyle and Tawney, it will be noticed, identify the market economy with society as a whole. They both consider that the market economy comprises or permeates the whole of society, and that in so doing it destroys relationships between people other than those contracted for economic purposes. Furthermore they assert that the society that has thus become identical with a market is one in which self-seeking, callousness and even downright maleficence are regarded as justified. But if, as I have indicated, the competitive market is only a part of any society in which it exists, then these criticisms are unacceptable. What would have to be shown is first, that where there is a market economy, it must permeate, and hence presumably corrupt, everything else in the society that harbours it. But second, even more fundamental than this is the claim that within the market itself men are necessarily dominated by avarice, lack of concern for others, and wish to harm them. Of course, if it is never right to look after one's own interests in competition with others, then the market economy must be fundamentally bad, since, as we have already indicated, all those participating in it are trying to do as well for themselves as they can.

This criticism must apply, not only to producing and merchanting firms, but to the ultimate consumers as well, for these aim to secure a consumer's surplus, that is, to make as large as possible the difference between what they pay in the market and what they would pay if they had to.[2] Thus we should not speak of profits as if they were, morally speaking, different

---

[1] These quotations are from p. 29 (Pelican edition, 1940 reprint); on p. 71 Tawney writes that in medieval times 'the problem of moralising economic life was faced and not abandoned'.

[2] Alfred Marshall *Principles of Economics* (9th edn, Macmillan, 1961), Book III, ch. vi. For subsequent discussion of the idea see 'Realism and relevance in consumer's surplus' by E. J. Mishan, in his *Welfare Economics. Five Introductory Essays* (New York, Random House, 1964). The great subtlety of the metaphysics of the theory is unnecessary for the point that the purchaser aims to do as well as he can for himself and is thus in the same moral boat as the profit-seeker.

from the advantages which all those who participate in the market economy hope to gain for themselves by selling, buying or working for a wage. The ultimate consumer is not generally as good at obtaining the advantages open to him as firms are good at making profits, for the purchasing of consumer goods is a less organised profession than it was in the days when most housewives specialised in it. But consumers' associations can bring expertise into the buying of consumer goods just as trade unions can advise and help men to make advantageous wage bargains. Profits, if they are honestly come by, indicate no more avarice than do wages and the purchases of shrewd and cautious buyers.

It might be objected that this only goes to show that in a competitive market economy all the participants, and not only those who set out to make profits, are engaged in self-interested activities which should be morally condemned. If the market were the whole of society this might be so, but the market is in practice an element in a society that extends far beyond it. Hence those who engage in market activities do so with aims that are related to the other aspects of the society in which they live. All men belong to a family, many of them have a religion, some of them have a care for social and philanthropic causes, an interest in art and science, a concern for their country. The interests they pursue in the market, therefore, are not merely private and personal, but are imbued with ambitions and predilections to which monetary success is often subordinate. Most men's market dealings are linked with their desire to provide for their families, but they may also be concerned to promote concerns connected with churches, clubs, voluntary societies and other groups to which they give their loyalty. Firms themselves are influenced by the outlooks of their directors and managers, and purchases by individuals manifest 'profiles' which vary from one to another. It is true that some people are so taken with the market that they want money for its own sake, and there are others who chiefly want to outdo other people. But they are hardly typical. What should be emphasised is that whatever their non-market aims, motives and ideals, they will not promote them by buying too dear or selling too cheap in market terms.

Tawney, in the passage I referred to above, writes as if the principle that a man should not take advantage of his neighbour's necessity is opposed to the market system. To establish and exploit, say, a monopoly of food during a famine would undoubtedly be immoral, but such monopolies, I suggest, go against the market system, and cannot be taken as typical unless it is the case that competitive markets *must* tend to develop into monopolies. Sickness and poverty among those who cannot help themselves may have to be dealt with outside the market mechanism,[1] which may, as Lord Robbins emphasised, have to be suspended in times of scarcity imposed, for example, by the siege conditions of war.[2] But this is not to say that in the course of market activities people are taking unfair or otherwise reprehensible advantage of one another. The market, as a method of recording consumer preferences and allocating resources can respond to any distribution or redistribution of income. In one sense, indeed, people *are* taking advantage of one another, and it is a very good thing that they do so. For in competitive markets people who need goods and services receive them from people who see advantage to themselves in providing them. To take advantage of people's necessities in this way is not morally reprehensible unless it is always wrong to require payment for goods provided or for services rendered. The better one meets the needs of others, the more profitable market activity becomes. This brings us to a crucial aspect of the morality of markets.

Economic harmonies and the 'invisible hand'

'Taking advantage of one's neighbour's necessity', we have seen, can mean two things. It can mean the exploitation by the strong of the weak or helpless by creating a monopoly and taking advantage of it; and it can mean the supplying for pay of goods and services that our neighbour wishes to buy. No one is going to defend exploitation by monopoly, but it should not be confused with responding to demand, and the question is whether the latter, which is the market method of helping one another, is to be morally condemned as well. Put in its very simplest terms, the question is: 'Is it always wrong to require

---

[1] The advantages claimed for the reversed income tax by Professor Milton Friedman is that it would redistribute income outside the market. *Capitalism and Freedom* (University of Chicago Press, 1962).

[2] Lionel Robbins. *The Economic Problem in Peace and War* (Macmillan, 1947).

payment for providing help?' The answer is undoubtedly 'No', and it is instructive to consider why.

Let us suppose a society in which there is division of labour and a belief among all its members that it is wrong to require payment for anything. In this society the man who grows potatoes wants to give them to those who need them, and the man who makes shoes wants to do the same. How do the potatoes and the shoes get to those who want them? Presumably these people go around and take some. But where do the potato-growers and shoemakers go for spades and leather? Has some kind man realised that these implements and materials will be needed and has he produced them for the potato-grower and the shoemaker? He would have to find out what sort they required, but what would happen if they did not like them? After all, there is something indelicate about criticising gifts. Nor can gifts be demanded either, and yet the potato-grower may need the spade when his friend is making one for some other friend who is breaking the ground for a much needed house.

Such considerations make it clear that a society with division of labour and limited resources cannot rely upon gifts to get its products distributed. Benevolence is good, but it is business that is needed, and business means mutual agreements, times of delivery, specifications and quantities, contracts, exchange and sales. These agreements and deals take place in order that people's needs shall be satisfied. But the satisfactions are reciprocal. Each producer needs the products of some or all the other producers, and some or all of them need what he produces. In producing for sale what he is good at producing, each producer supplies the others with what they want. The buyer, unlike a recipient of gifts, can require the producer to make what is wanted. The producer or seller, unlike a bestower of gifts, is led to supply the types and quantities needed at times when they are of use.

This, I suggest, is what ought to be meant by the system of economic harmony. It is not that each individual seeks his own interest and that some 'invisible hand', to use Adam Smith's famous expression, sees to it that this results in benefits for all. For such a hand might lose its cunning or become paralysed. It is rather that the very structure or system of free exchange in a society with division of labour and limited resources is one in which what each party produces is for some others to have in return for what the producer would like to have from them. Benefiting oneself by providing what others need is the *raison d'être* of the whole affair. It is not that the good of others is a contingent byproduct of selfishness, but that each party can only benefit himself by benefiting others. He may from time to time benefit others without benefiting himself, by making gifts, or what comes to the same thing in a market, by selling below what he knows to be the market price. But persistently to do this would be to opt out of the system, the very functioning of which requires service to be by exchange rather than by gift. If there is to be business, it had better be business.

In *The Wealth of Nations*[1] Adam Smith seems to be recommending the method of exchange on the ground that it is better for an able-bodied man who wants what others have, to offer something in exchange for it rather than 'by every servile and fawning attention to obtain their good will'. He also suggests in the same passage that the methods of the beggar are not likely to be consistently successful, human selfishness being what it is, that they would lead to a great waste of time, and that they neither do nor can 'provide him with them ["the necessaries of life"] as he has occasion for them'. The last two seem to me to be the really compelling reasons, as they would still apply, as I have suggested above, even if human beings were primarily and fundamentally altruistic. For the system to work, even altruistic people have to look to their own benefit. Does this mean that they have to make themselves selfish? Not at all. What it means is that, whatever their outlook or their temperament, they must try to look after themselves while they play their part in the competitive market system. If they are honest and honourable men the part they play will be in keeping with their character. If they are not, they may still be kept in line by fear of the law or their knowledge that others will not do business with them if they are suspected of double-dealing. If they are misanthropic, they may try to forget that they cannot benefit themselves without providing other people with things they want to have. But if they provide what others do not want they will find themselves out of business.

[1] Book i, ch. 2.

The system was described very well in the eighteenth century by Le Mercier de la Rivière when he wrote:

It is of the essence of [this] order that the particular interest of each individual can never be separated from the common interest of all; we find a very convincing proof of this in the complete freedom which ought to obtain in trade, if property is not to be damaged. The personal interest which this great freedom encourages, strongly and continually urges every individual to improve, to multiply the things that he wishes to sell; in this way to enlarge the mass of enjoyments which he can provide for other men, in order to enlarge by this means, the enjoyments that other men can provide for him in exchange. Thus *the world goes by itself* (va de lui-même); the desire for enjoyment and the freedom to enjoy, never ceasing to induce the multiplication of products and the growth of industry, impress on the whole of the society a motion which becomes a perpetual tendency towards its best possible condition.[1]

We may no longer share the eighteenth-century writer's optimistic belief that all this will lead to 'the best possible condition', nor have we yet considered the relation of the analysis to freedom. But the central position, it seems to me, is correct, that is, the claim that in competitive markets individuals, whether firms or persons, provide for others in working for themselves. We might equally well say that in working for others they work for themselves. Hence, someone who was averse to helping other people would, once he understood the logic of the system, be rather disconcerted if he had to play a part in it. For business success depends on supplying people with what they want, and hence involves helping them.

It may still be objected that there is something paradoxical about the morality of urging people to act selfishly in order to promote the common good, for, it may be said, while someone is deliberately pursuing the common good he cannot be acting selfishly, and while he is acting selfishly he cannot be deliberately promoting the common good. Is there any real difference, it may be asked, between advising people to look after themselves on the one hand, and asking them to look after themselves in order to promote the common good on the other? Will not this be taken, and rightly so, as an invitation not to bother about other people? Historians of the subject say that Adam Smith was influenced by Mandeville's paradox that

[1] Le Mercier de la Rivière *L'Ordre Naturel et Essentiel des Sociétés Politiques* (London, 1767), Vol. 2, p. 444. The passage occurs in a chapter describing the benefits of commerce. It is quoted by J. R. McCulloch in his 'Introductory Discourse' to his edition of *The Wealth of Nations*, fifth edition, 1863; first edition, 1828.

private vices are public virtues when he argued that an 'invisible hand' secured a result, viz. the interest of the society, that the individual had not intended. The word 'intend' was not very fortunately chosen by Smith, for we can hardly intend something as remote as the interest of the society, we can only aim at it or try to bring it about. What we intend are things much closer to us than the interest of the society. When we intend to do something it is something we think we know quite well how to do. Again, when Smith says 'It is not from the benevolence of the butcher, the brewer, or the baker that we expect our dinner, but from their regard to their own interest',[1] he is right but a little misleading, for in a competitive market economy these people do try to give their customers what they want. They must try to do this if they are to sell their goods. The word 'benevolence' suggests gratuitous or unremunerated help, and certainly butchers do not give their meat away. But remunerated help is help nevertheless, and the point of trading in a market is that the help that men can afford one another is extended over a wide area and rendered more efficient by the device of free exchange. Giving help and receiving it are united in one process. Not only is self-help rewarded, but misanthropy is rendered difficult by being made to result in self-injury.

The market and its limits

From time to time ministers of religion assert that religion ought not to be confined to church and to private life and call for the application of Christian principles of conduct to economic affairs. More generally, critics of the market economy often say that moral principles should be applied throughout society and not only in the non-market sections of it. This is Tawney's view when, in the passage quoted above (p. 12), he contrasts the 'view of economic activity which regarded it as one among other kinds of moral conduct' with 'the view of it as dependent upon impersonal and almost automatic forces'. The suggestion is that there is an impersonal system going on like clockwork— and we here recall Le Mercier de la Rivière's world that 'goes on its own'—with no kind of moral conduct in it, and a world quite distinct from the economic world, in which moral conduct does occur.

[1] *The Wealth of Nations*, Book 1, ch. 2.

But if Tawney's words mean what they say, then they certainly say one thing that is wrong, for it is obvious that moral conduct, in the sense of conduct that is morally right or wrong and is in general subject to moral standards, does take place in the market as it is and does not need to be imported into it. For in the market people can be just or unjust, honest or dishonest, reliable or unreliable, and these are moral characteristics. They can also be cautious or rash, and these may be regarded as moral characteristics too, although some might say that they belong to the sphere of prudence and its opposite rather than to morality. Whether or not we say that prudence belongs to the moral sphere, there is not necessarily anything *wrong* in it, and hence there is nothing necessarily wrong in the looking after one's interests that the market calls for. The suggestion, therefore, that people must be immoral or amoral in their market activities is quite unfounded, for, even if prudence is not to count among moral virtues, honestly undoubtedly must. If it is argued that it is not genuine honesty because it is enforced by legal or professional sanctions, the answer is that genuine honesty is no more removed from the world of business because there are penalties for cheating, than genuine love is removed from the non-business world because there are penalties for assault.

On examination, therefore, we find that there is absolutely nothing in the complaint that markets are by their very nature immoral or amoral,[1] although many of those who participate in them cheat or would cheat if they dared. All that remains to charge the market with on this score, therefore, is that in it the Christian virtues of humility, charity and self-sacrifice are not displayed, or are displayed markedly less than in the political management of the economy.

But how could humility, charity and self-sacrifice be shown in the market? If we ask how they could be exercised by business firms, the absurdity of the question becomes apparent. A firm can give away money that might otherwise have been distributed as profits, but it must be in a financial position to do this if it is not to fall into financial difficulties. The very idea of a firm showing humility or sacrificing itself is absurd, and the idea of these virtues being exercised by individual participants

[1] Some are, of course, such as markets in men, love, scandal.

in the market is hardly less so. If a man constantly deferred to others and could not bring himself to accept an order if someone else would thereby fail to get it, he could not long survive in business. We shall have more to say about this when we discuss the morality of competition, but it should be pretty clear already that no one who does not try to make a profit, or, what is the same thing, to avoid a loss, can effectively take part in market activities. Nor can he long remain in a position to make gifts to good causes or be taxed for any means whatever.

But this does not mean that even the Christian virtues must be absent from the business world altogether. Between the members of a firm or between its employees there is plenty of scope for humility and charity, and perhaps even for self-sacrifice as well. For example, a man might allow a friend to be promoted to a position which he would have liked to occupy himself. But this, although it happened in the business world, would not in itself be a market activity. There just would be no sense in a firm's allowing another firm to take its business from it. I hardly think, either, that we should regard it as humility or self-sacrifice if an employee took no steps to prevent his employer from underpaying him, unless his employer were a friend or a charity which the employee hoped to help thereby. Furthermore, those expending funds for good causes have a duty to make their expenditures as economically effective as possible.

In *Unto this Last* (1862), Ruskin says that it is the duty of a soldier to die rather than to leave his post in battle, of a physician to die rather than to leave his post in a plague, of a pastor to die rather than to teach falsehood, of a lawyer to die rather than to countenance injustice. Then Ruskin asks: 'The merchant—what is *his* due occasion of death?' His answer is that the merchant's function is to provide for society and that he must therefore face death or damage 'rather than fail in any engagement, or consent to any deterioration, adulteration, or unjust exorbitant price of that which he provides'. Furthermore, the merchant must so conduct his business as to promote the welfare of his employees: 'And so it becomes his duty, not only to be always considering how to produce what he sells in the purest and cheapest forms, but how to make the various employments involved in the production, or the transference of it, most beneficial to the men employed.'

The comparison of the merchant and the industrialist with the soldier was repeated by Tawney in *The Acquisitive Society*:

The idea that there is some mysterious difference between making munitions of war and firing them, between building schools and teaching in them when built, between providing food and providing health, which makes it at once inevitable and laudable that the former should be carried on with a single eye to pecuniary gain, while the latter are conducted by professional men, who expect to be paid for their services, but who neither watch for windfalls nor raise their fees merely because there are more sick to be cured, more children to be taught, or more enemies to be resisted, is an illusion only less astonishing than that the leaders of industry should welcome the insult as an honour and wear their humiliation as a kind of halo. The work of making boots or building a house is in itself no more degrading than that of curing the sick or teaching the ignorant. It is as necessary and therefore as honourable. It should be at least equally bound by rules which have as their object to maintain the standards of professional service. It should be at least equally free from the vulgar subordination of moral standards to financial interests.[1]

This passage occurs in the course of a section headed: 'Industry as a profession'. Like Ruskin, Tawney contrasts businessmen, whose aim is to make profits, with professional men who do not 'watch for windfalls'. Industry, he says, is organised for the protection of rights, 'mainly rights to pecuniary gain', a profession 'for the performance of *duties*', the measure of their success being 'the service which they perform, not the gains which they amass'.[2] Thus, the suggestion is that if professional men acted on commercial principles, doctors would raise their fees during epidemics, teachers would demand more pay when the numbers of their pupils increased, and soldiers would do the same in time of war. The argument based on this suggestion is that since doctors, teachers and soldiers would regard it as wrong to do these things, businessmen should behave more like professional men and look to other things besides pecuniary gain. Curing the sick, it is said, counts most for the doctor, getting children to think and to exercise skills counts most for the teacher, defending the country counts most for the soldier. By analogy, therefore, supplying the needs of his customers should count most for the businessman who should not, therefore, have 'a single eye to pecuniary gain'. We must now proceed to examine the analogy and the argument.

[1] *The Acquisitive Society* (Bell, 1921), Fontana edition (1961), pp. 91–2.
[2] *Ibid.*, p. 89.

Business and the professions

There are so many different factors involved in these comparisons that it is very difficult to disentangle the essential from the irrelevant. Professions, for example, are very much concerned with their members' rights, and trades and industries and firms have to recognise all sorts of duties to suppliers, customers and employees. This was so in 1921, when Tawney was writing, as well as today, and hardly seems to present a fruitful topic for examination. As the businessman is compared with a number of different professions, perhaps it will be best if we first consider his side of the comparison.

Does the businessman have 'a single eye for pecuniary gain'? From what we have said about the competitive enterprise system this is true, in so far as the businessman is in business to avoid losses or to make a profit. If he gives anything away, this, unless it is a part of his marketing activity, is outside his business dealings, the very point of which is that he gets what he can by supplying goods and services that are in demand. What he can get is determined by what the buyers can and will pay and by the quality of his goods by comparison with that of the goods offered by other suppliers. He is required to be honest, to keep his promises about dates of delivery, to refrain from misdescribing his goods. He is not called upon to die for his customers, although keeping his promises to them may require him to work very hard on their behalf as well as on his own—and in a competitive system, in doing the latter he will be doing the former as well.[1] A lazy distributor of insulin or of 'heart machines' is not only unbusinesslike but also insensitive or callous.

Now let us suppose that there is a shortage, not of his contriving, of the goods that a merchant supplies. This will bring the price up, but it may not bring more profit to the merchant, for the volume of his sales may diminish. If there were a very serious shortage and the price went high, the poorer customers might have to buy less or nothing at all. If, however, the suppliers did not put up the price, the goods would be bought

[1] In an overstretched economy suffering from wage inflation, he will not be able to *keep* his promises about deliveries, and if he does not *make* the promises he will not get the orders. This is one way in which inflation corrodes basic morality. To compare the selfishness of business men with the public spirit of professional men in such circumstances is fatuous, but it is only fair to mention that Tawney had in mind quite a different set of economic conditions in a non-inflationary economy.

up by the earliest buyers, probably those who first realised that there was a shortage. If in such conditions there was only one supplier, he might be able to make very high profits, especially if there were no substitutes for the products he sells. The profits of each would be limited if there were competition between the sellers. If the shortage were a general shortage of food it would be considered wrong to allow the demand to push the prices up to such an extent that the poorer people were brought to starvation or near to it, and in such circumstances a publicly controlled system of rationing would be introduced. A new law, penalties for breach of it, the registration of individuals, the issue of ration books would then become necessary.

We may now examine the contrasting cases cited by Tawney. The doctors he had in mind are supposed to be working privately for fees. What happens when there is an epidemic? Tawney assumes that they would not think it right to put up their fees. But they would then have to see more patients and would in consequence receive *more* in fees, even though the fees had not been raised. But perhaps the epidemic is so great that not all patients can be treated by the existing body of doctors. Then each doctor would be expected to treat those who needed treatment most, as far as he could find this out. It is important to notice that he can judge the varying needs of his patients much more easily than a shopkeeper could judge the varying needs of his customers, for the doctor examines the patient, even goes into his home, whereas the shopkeeper, unless he serves a village, does not know much about the personal circumstances of his customers. Hence a doctor can act as his own rationing authority and, indeed, might be *better* at it that any Ministry of Health. Treating patients is a very different sort of service from selling goods, and the differences between what is reasonable from shopkeepers and merchants in times of famine and what is reasonable from doctors in times of epidemics depend on this distinction. Perhaps a reason why traders are criticised in times of famine more than doctors are in times of epidemic is that the former can often get food for themselves whereas doctors run the same risks of disease as everyone else, if not more.

We need not consider the case of doctors employed by a national health service, as the comparisons we need may be examined by relation to teachers and soldiers, the other cases mentioned by Ruskin and Tawney. According to Tawney, then, teachers would not consider it right to demand salary increases in return for teaching more children. But if this meant that they would have to work much harder, it would not be wrong of them to make such a demand and the increased salary may be essential to attract more people into teaching and away from other employments. The difference between teachers and traders is largely due to differences in what they do. Teachers have continuous personal relationships with considerable numbers of children, and are bound to them by likes (and dislikes) and by their understanding of their characters and personalities. They are expected to give encouragement and to have sympathy and loyalty. These are not qualities much required in the processes of marketing, and businessmen exercise them, if at all, in their relation to colleagues within the firm. What is necessarily central in the activity of teaching is peripheral in the activity of trading. Hence it is inappropriate that the professional attitudes of teachers should find their way into industry and commerce, even though in business certain teaching functions are necessary here and there. It is worth noticing, too, that whereas a teacher's pupils are, so to say, his final products, the businessman's subordinates are links in a chain of production and distribution.

The comparison with soldiers raises some points of interest. It would be disgraceful for soldiers to demand more pay in time of war with the threat of not fighting at all unless the increase was granted. Yet the trader will not forgo a rise of price in times of scarcity. But for the trader's action in not raising prices to have any point he would have to ration his supplies, and his customers might not like that at all—he needs the authority of the state to do such things. The soldier is part of the state's authority, and if he refuses to fight he mutinies, and if he does so successfully, he seizes authority from its former holders. Why should not the merchant risk his life for something or other as the soldier risks his life for his country? Under a system of division of labour the merchant's circumstances do not generally require this. His function is to take another sort of risk, that of financing a transaction before its total costs are known and before the demand from customers is known either. The soldier is housed and fed and clothed by the state, while the entrepreneur takes the responsibility for these things himself and faces economic uncertainties. Here, again, therefore, the idea of transferring the responsibilities of a soldier to the man of business is seen to rest on similarities too slight to produce any conviction, once the negative analogies are brought to light.

It is absurd, then, to criticise the man of business for not exhibiting the devotion of a hard-working doctor, the sympathy of a schoolteacher, or the self-sacrifice of a soldier. His circumstances do not normally call for these virtues, but for foresight, honesty, reliability in keeping promises, and a readiness to accept the consequences of the risks he has to take.

Is private trading wicked?

It may be argued that we have still failed to identify the central moral defect of profit-making, which is to be found in the very process of bargaining itself. There is, it may be said, something essentially ignoble in the higgling of the market. Traders are engaged in wicked work. We are not surprised to find such an attitude in the writings of Plato and of other upholders of an aristocratic form of society, for trading has always been looked down upon by the nobility, who use traders and sometimes have pillaged them. But why should this aristocratic attitude survive into presentday society? Can any convincing reasons be put forward in support of it?

The best attempt to do this that I know of was that of J. A. Hobson. One of Hobson's earliest books was his *John Ruskin* (1898), in which he expounded and upheld Ruskin's economic theories. In his later writings Hobson applied Ruskin's ideas about non-economic goods to the social problems of the nineteen-twenties and nineteen-thirties, and endeavoured to show that dealings in markets are essentially bad. In *Wealth and Life* (Macmillan, 1929) Hobson wrote:

Save in the rare cases when both parties are equally strong in finance, knowledge and organisation, business bargains distribute the gain unequally and proportionately to an economic force which, in its final issue, means the power 'to starve the other out' (pp. 211–12).

In the same passage he also wrote:

By their very nature the bargaining processes inhibit the consideration of the good of others, and concentrate the mind and will of each party upon the bargaining for his own immediate and material gains . . . this constant drive of selfish interest involves a hardening of the moral arteries (p. 213).

And in a lecture entitled *The Moral Challenge to the Economic System*, given to the Ethical Union in 1933, he said:

Sometimes the market is favourable to the sellers, sometimes to the buyers. What does that mean? It means that a superior bargaining power belongs to one side or the other, and that the price will be determined by this superiority of power, distributing the gain not with equity but force (p. 15).

Let us first consider the claim that in market dealings it is 'force' or 'power' that prevails over 'equity'. Does force or power prevail in practice? Certainly not in the sense in which it would prevail if, instead of there being an exchange or sale, the stronger party had taken from the weaker party what he wanted from him. Markets can only operate when force of this sort (what Bastiat called 'spoliation') has been eliminated. Competitive markets require law and peace and order if they are to work at all. Thus, 'power' and 'force' must mean something else, 'the power to starve the other out' mentioned by Hobson in *Wealth and Life*. But no such power is exercised when the prices of cabbages, meat, bread and other foods are settled in ordinary markets. Of course, the producers and owners of these things need not sell them and could, if they could concert to stop all rival suppliers, hold them back until their customers got really hungry. But the producers and merchants are in business to sell, and if one firm tried to make its customers feel the pinch of hunger, other firms would sell to them. In a competitive market a price, so to say, *emerges*, by reference to the demand and to the available supply. If someone cannot pay the market price, then he has to go without, and hence the very poor cannot satisfy their needs as well as the rich can satisfy theirs and may have to be given additional money. Force is present in that if the very poor tried to *take* what they could not *buy*, they would face arrest and punishment. But if very many were in this position, the price would have to come down, otherwise the goods would not be sold. It should not be forgotten that not only do consumers wish (or need) to have, but that producers and merchants want to sell. Furthermore, employers may have fixed capital investment at stake, whereas their employees can walk out and leave them with the consequences.

Force or power are much more apparent, I suggest, when there is *no* market, as when governments in time of war barter large quantities of goods or contract bulk sales and purchases with governments of other countries. In such circumstances there cannot be a market and, as experience showed in the last war, the parties finally settle because they have to.[1] Even so, it is not necessarily the *stronger* that gets his way. For the weaker party can bargain from its very weakness, arguing, sometimes successfully, that the stronger power has more to lose in the event of the weaker power's collapsing. So called 'oriental' bargaining, again, is either a form of amusement, or else possible only because one or both of the parties is ignorant of the state of the market. In developed competitive markets there is very little bargaining because there is no need for it among those who understand the supply situation.

I suggest, therefore, that Hobson's account of bargaining in a market is more like bargaining in the absence of markets. It is indeed, more like politics than trade, and one must conclude that, in spite of his discoveries about the effects of over-saving, he did not really know what goes on in markets.[2]

Another element in Hobson's indictment of the market is that the price is not determined by equity. By this he means that the market price is not a just price. The passage we have quoted from his Ethical Union lecture suggests that Hobson thought that a price would be just, or at any rate less unjust, when there is no large discrepancy in bargaining power between buyers and sellers. It is certainly an appealing picture of economic justice that Hobson sets before us, in which no one is under pressure from anyone else and everyone exerts the same economic influence as all the others. In order that such a situation could exist, it would be necessary for no one to be so poor that he paid prices that he regretted having to pay. In such a situation, sellers too would not be forced to receive less than their goods had cost them. There would be no shortages, no commercial miscalculations, no governmental muddles, no

---

[1] At that time the Russians searched through Western trade journals to find the highest prices quoted in them for the commodities they wished to sell.

[2] His interesting *Confessions of an Economic Heretic* (Allen & Unwin, 1939) bears this out. Hobson lived in the world of books and journalism and was sheltered by a private income. He complains that no university department of economics in the country ever *asked* him to take a job with them, but he does not say that he ever *applied* for one.

obstinate or arbitrary men making use of an advantageous position. That is, in order that just prices could be established supplies would have to be ample and yet not constitute a glut, and a population of reasonable, moderate men, free from inordinate desires, would have to be in possession of incomes that made them invulnerable to economic pressures. This may be an ideal situation; it is neither a real nor a likely one. The prices established in a competitive market have the function of getting goods and services from suppliers to consumers in the conditions that prevail. With increasing prosperity these prices might get established with less urgent pressures on the parties involved and so approach nearer to Hobson's conception of justice. But to complain that they are not just in this sense is to refer to an unavoidable consequence of the world's scarcities and man's imperfection.

In a part of his Ethical Union lecture which I have not quoted, Hobson shows that a major injustice in the settling of market prices which he has in mind, is the price paid for labour. The 'vital resources' of employers, he argues, are larger than those of their employees, so that employees are forced by their employers to accept lower wages than they would do if they had no fear of losing their jobs. Hence, it is wage bargaining in a competitive market which he considers to lead to particularly unjust results.

Hobson was writing at a time when there was much unemployment and when, therefore, employees were at a disadvantage because the employer could generally find someone else to do the job if the employee were disposed to press his demands. But the position now is very different. When there is less unemployment and when most employees are ready (or are persuaded) to strike when their unions require them to do so, the bargaining advantage is on the side of the wage-earners. According to Hobson's view of justice, therefore, at a time of full or overfull employment it would be employers who are unjustly treated, and justice can only be made possible when employment is less than full, and in consequence employers have a prospect of resisting some of the claims the unions make upon them. His notion of a just wage, therefore, comes very close to that of a wage established in a competitive market between parties who have alternative bargains open to them;

in this case, between employees who can offer their services elsewhere and employers who can hold their employees to their agreements without thereby risking a strike. It is interesting to note that Professor Michael Fogarty, in his defence of the scholastic theory of the just wage, assumes a fairly freely working labour market in which monopolistic and monopsonistic positions are not exploited.[1]

Another difference between Hobson's day and ours is that unemployment benefits are now less inadequate, and receiving them is not regarded as a stigma. To this extent, the employee is under less pressure in making his wage bargain and is therefore less forced than in the past. His choice is not now between accepting the employer's terms or starving and becoming an object of contempt. It is rather between working for a higher remuneration or striking and receiving strike pay himself and state assistance for his family He might even find another job while the strike is on. Leaving moral considerations out of account, a man might opt for leisure and lower remuneration rather than for work with higher remuneration In so far as fear of unemployment is fear of idleness or of loss of dignity, it presupposes the value and dignity of work and of providing for oneself and one's family. If voluntary unemployment and idleness ceased altogether to be regarded as disgraceful, and if it were legally possible and sufficiently well provided for, wage bargaining would be of interest only to the more energetic, ambitious and conscientious members of the community. Trade unions, therefore, have a material interest in the dignity of labour, and stand to lose their functions if it is belittled or denied.

Profits and wages

It is implied in the Carlyle–Ruskin–Tawney–Hobson line of thought that profits are morally inferior types of remuneration by comparison with professional fees or wages and salaries. In a free and competitive system profits are obtained by laying out monies in buying or producing goods and selling them when they are produced or demanded. The entrepreneur has to buy materials, engage workmen, pay for transport, cover the

[1] M. Fogarty, *The Just Wage* (London, G. Chapman, 1961), see esp. pp. 12 and 264–5.

costs of all this and recoup them by the sales he makes. He runs the risk of not recouping his outgoings, for he may have paid too readily or too highly, or the goods he has bought or has been responsible for manufacturing may no longer be in demand, or may be less in demand than when he set the transaction in motion He contracts to sell his goods or products, but he contracts with no one to give him a profit and he may in the event make a loss. Whether or not he makes a profit, and its amount if he does make one, depend on his skill in forecasting and in organising, and on luck as well.[1] The entrepreneur has to be willing to back his judgment and chance his luck Like someone who backs horses, he hopes to strike lucky but, again like him, he may fail.

Wages and salaries are very different. The employee has to find an entrepreneur, or a public firm or corporation, who will employ him. He then contracts for a wage or salary for a certain period. He is remunerated for doing particular sorts of things in an already existing organisation which he does not control. His remuneration is something prescribed for a definite period. By contracting for it, he is on to a near-certainty for the period of the contract,[2] but he has no hope of striking lucky as the entrepreneur might do. In a letter dated 25 September 1857, Marx asserts that wages were, in their first beginnings, payments known as *peculium castrense*, service money, paid to soldiers in the Roman army. I doubt whether he is right in this, but it does bring out an important feature of wages and salaries, namely that they are payments made by an employer to those who serve or work for him. There is someone definite who pays out the wages contracted for. Profits, on the contrary, are what are left over when this man or firm has completed the transaction of making, moving, selling the goods.

These differences are of central importance. If all remuneration were by means of wages and salaries, everyone would have to be employed by some individual or by some firm or corporation. In these circumstances there would be no individual entrepreneurs at all. Could there then be individual firms? Hardly, for what would a firm be in the absence of possible

---

[1] Inflation lessens his risks and makes it easier for him to make profits.

[2] The employee takes a risk when he acquires a skill, which at some later date, may not be needed.

profit or loss? Suppose there were several 'organisations', as we might call them, providing the same type of goods, say shoes, and suppose they were not trying to make a profit. What output would they decide on? Who would their customers be? How would they fix their prices? In the absence of the test of profitability, the firms would have to make these decisions by agreement between one another, or, if they could not agree, someone would have to tell them what to do.[1] If firms cannot make profits and losses, they must become administrative or productive units within an organisation where everyone is paid for his services to it. Profits, therefore, belong and are essential to independently operating economic units, wages and salaries to those who serve them or who serve other bodies such as armies or nationalised concerns. Profits are bound up with one main system of economic organisation. Wages are payable under all except slave systems. Profits are not contracted for, wages are. Profits have no definite limits, up or down. Wages have as their lower limit what is necessary to keep the wage-earner alive and fit and willing to work, and as their upper limit what an employer would be prepared to pay rather than do without the wage-earner's services.

Because of these fundamental differences, one would expect wages and profits to carry different moral implications. Wages are contracted for, and therefore impose specific duties on those who pay them and those who receive them. The former must endeavour to pay the same wages for the same work, the latter to do the work they get the wages for doing. Since profits are not contracted for, there can be no very definite idea of a just or fair profit. Profits are essentially residual, variable, problematic. To use the word 'remuneration' both for wages and for profits is to suggest that they are more alike than they really are. The profit-seeker has expectations and hopes but can make no claim to any particular rate of profit. The wage and salary earner can claim what was agreed on and what is appropriate for the amount of work he does. To apply to profits the moral principles that are applied to wages is to abolish, or to wish to abolish, profits altogether, and that would be to abolish or wish to abolish the system of competing firms and

[1] In centrally directed societies they are told by the state, although in recent years such societies are finding it necessary to use the profit and price system.

entrepreneurs in favour of a universal employer or combination of employers.

At a period of continuing inflation, a large proportion of entrepreneurs and firms make profits, and very few fail to do so. As a result, the risk-taking aspect of profits appears to be diminished and they appear more like fees or wages. Furthermore, when governments intervene in the fixing of wages and prices their accountants, in arriving at the levels they propose, are bound to think of a level of profits which firms may be reasonably expected to make. In consequence, profits are made to appear more like fees or discounts than they are under conditions of competition. Again, when politicians dispute on the hustings about the distribution of wealth and the level of incomes, they tend to lump profits and wages together, as competing forms of remuneration. When the 'pay-freeze' of 20 July 1966 was instituted the government said it must apply to dividends as well as to wages, even though they were aware that the deflationary steps they were taking would reduce or eliminate many profits in any case. When government intervention leads to the conception of 'reasonable' profits, then governments and the firms that feel bound to cooperate with them imply that a profit is something to which a firm has a *right*, or to which it is *entitled*, something that can be *fixed by agreement*. But a profit then becomes more like a fee or a discount, and the whole structure of industry is being looked at in a different light.[1] For the 'profit' is now regarded as a cost of the enterprise, as something that must be allowed for, even if not paid out, like interest or bank loans, or like wages.

We shall consider this further when we examine the ethics of systems alternative to the competitive market economy. In the meantime it is sufficient to notice that, since profits are not rights or entitlements, they are, morally as well as legally, very different from wages, and different, though not as different as wages are, from fees and discounts.

[1] As in H. F. R. Catherwood's *Britain with the Brakes Off* (Hodder & Stoughton, 1966). It is significant that the Director-General of the NEDC, who wishes to draw business men into a state-controlled system tends to write of 'return on capital' when others would say 'profit', and to emphasise the weaknesses of competition.

III. The Ethics of Competition

Competition, strife and rivalry

Critics of competitive markets often contrast the competition that is essential to such markets with non-competitive cooperation. They believe that competition goes along with such characteristics as aggression, emulation, rivalry, conflict and strife, and that cooperation belongs with mutual aid, benevolence, modesty and harmony. In their view it follows, therefore, that economic competition is morally inferior to cooperative, non-competitive modes of commercial and industrial organisation. Right-minded people, it is assumed, are against strife and in favour of harmony and mutual aid. Modestly conducted cooperation, therefore, is superior to aggressive competition, and hence collectivist organisation is to be preferred to what these critics call 'the law of the jungle'. Collectivists are on the side of the angels while supporters of competitive markets are the Devil's disciples, helping him to bring misfortunes on the hindmost. Some, even, of those who support capitalism do so in a shamefaced way,[1] as they are convinced that in itself collectivism, being a form of cooperation and harmony, is morally superior to capitalism, even though, alas, human egoism makes capitalism inevitable.

We must now ask whether competition in free markets does have the morally obnoxious features we have just mentioned. Is it a species of strife, rivalry, emulation? Is it opposed to altruism, cooperation and harmony? Is the only moral justification for competitive markets and capitalism that socialism is an ideal beyond human capacity to realise?

According to Dr Samuel Johnson, competition is 'the action of endeavouring to gain what another endeavours to gain at the same time'. Johnson expresses this definition in morally neutral terms and brings out the central idea that in competition two

---

[1] See again Catherwood, *Britain with the Brakes Off*. In *The Christian in Industrial Society* (London, Tyndale, 1964) Mr Catherwood had proposed the setting up of what were later called 'Little Neddies' (p. 37).

or more people want and try to get what only one can have. He does not say anything about *how* they try to get it, since this depends upon what it is that they want and how it *can* be got. There certainly are what we might call competitive jungle situations in which animals seize food and run away with it or fight among themselves for it. Human beings sometimes do similar things, as when the members of a Bingo Club jostled each other as they pillaged presents intended for children at a Christmas party. Those who gain them do so as a result of strength or agility, but although some animals fight to the death, human beings generally confine their scramble within rules. With animals there may be no rules at all, and no conception of what is fair or unfair.[1] When 'all's fair in love or war' human beings approach the jungle situation.

But let us now consider the sort of situation in which human beings compete for a prize or a job. In such situations the competitors may not meet one another and may not even know one another. When a prize is offered, say, for the best essay on Balzac or for the first correct solution of a mathematical problem, the winner of the competition is the competitor who does the required thing best or first. There has to be an awarding authority which makes the award according to certain rules. The essay has to be of such and such a length and has to be sent in by such and such a date. Applicants for a job have to submit accounts of their qualifications, specimens of their work, and so on. If there is only one prize or only one job, then at least one competitor has to be unsuccessful.

We may now compare prize competition situations with competitive jungle situations. In the latter, let us suppose, there are no rules and no awarding authorities. In the absence of rules, jungle competition may take place when there is enough for all, even though it is intensified when there is a scarcity. In prize competition situations, there is never enough for all, and there must be losers. Jungle competition often takes place by means of fighting, but this is not necessary to it, since by eating its food or occupying its space, a group of animals may destroy another group it does not come into contact with. For competition of either sort to involve rivalry, the competitors

---

[1] Animals do generally confine their fights within rules, and so may be said to have some conception of what is permissible.

have to know one another, for when 'rivalry' does not mean the same thing as 'competition', it means the attempt of individuals or groups to outdo other individuals or groups, and this requires the rivals to have some knowledge of one another. It is possible to compete without knowing that one is competing, for someone might endeavour to obtain a prize or job without knowing that others are after it too. The essence of competition is that each competitor strives after what he wants. The essence of rivalry is that each competitor strives to outdo the others. In competition, the failure of the losers is a consequence of the success of the winners, not something that the winners aim to secure. Rivals, on the other hand, set out to *defeat each other* as well as to win the prize. To aim at defeating someone else comes somewhat closer to malevolence than mere competition does. Someone who endeavours to write the best essay in order to win the prize, may have no desire to defeat anyone else, but rivals do endeavour to defeat one another. Friendly rivalry is possible, as in games, but even this can easily spill over into hostility.

In jungle competition, then, the competing parties may fight, and may act as rivals to one another. But even in this primitive kind of competition, fighting *need* not occur, and does not when a species of animal unwittingly destroys the food of another species. In prize or job competition, there is an awarding authority proceeding according to rules, as there is not in jungle competition. As in some sorts of jungle competition, the competitors for prizes or jobs may not know one another or have any personal contact with one another. If they know one another they can behave as rivals. Rivals can be friends, as in games, but rivalry has kinship with hostility and malevolence, because rivals endeavour to outdo one another as well as to do what will win them the prize. The existence of rules for competitions for prizes and jobs limits the things that can be done to win. Competitors at local flower shows have been known to destroy their rivals' blooms. But this sort of behaviour is against the rules.

How, then, is economic competition related to the forms of competition we have now considered? It shares one important presupposition with them, that there is not an abundance of everything for everybody. If everyone could always get everything that he wanted, there would be no economic activity and no competition. Competition of all sorts presupposes scarcity, or at any rate a *belief* that what is wanted is scarce. (There might be enough food for all the animals who fight for it, but they fight because they do not know this.) Now competitive markets are not places where people fight, nor places where they pursue their rivalries. We have already seen that the attempts to outwit one another in what is called 'oriental' bargaining are not features of developed markets, but can only make sense for parties who are ignorant of conditions of supply and demand. Rivalry comes in when political considerations are important, as with pre-emptive purchases in time of war. But in general, economic behaviour in competitive markets is a peaceful sort of thing. Piracy and confiscation are uncommercial activities and trade flourishes when goods can be inspected and moved about without danger from marauding bands. Exchange, as we have seen, is morally preferable to spoliation or entreaty.

These, however, are very general considerations, and we must now consider some forms of economic activity in more detail, in order to see what morally relevant forms economic competition may take. Let us consider, then, competition between firms for a contract, competition in the labour market, and competition to sell to ultimate consumers.

(a) Competition for contracts

When firms compete for a contract they are in a situation analogous to that between competitors for a prize or a job. Each firm tries to get the order for itself by considering its own technical resources and probable costs in relation to what it considers the ordering firm is willing to pay. Its knowledge that other firms are tendering discourages it from asking too much, and its desire to make as good a profit as possible makes it unwilling to ask too little. Knowledge, intelligence and luck all affect the success of the enterprise. Rivalry need not enter into the situation at all, although, of course, it often does. A spirit of rivalry could cloud the judgment of a firm or individual and lead to unprofitable courses. In trying to obtain an order, of course, the tendering firm does more than quote its price, it will laud its product. Its representative may entertain the potential buyer and flatter him. But a buyer who signs a contract because of the charm of the salesman rather than because of the economic merits of the deal may come to regret it and certainly will do so if he makes a practice of acting in that way. Both parties will judge the success of the contract in terms of eventual profit or loss and, in a competitive situation, are led by the hope of profit to cut their costs as much as they can.

It should be noted that there is impersonal competition between firms, just as there is impersonal competition between animals in the jungle. We have said that a group or species of animal, even without fighting, may deprive another group or species of its food or space, and in so doing may lead to its extinction. In the process of natural selection those animals which do not succeed in adapting themselves to their circumstances eventually die out. They may be devoured by others, or they may just be deprived of what they need by others which do not ever meet or recognise them. Something analogous happens between firms. A firm which makes and uses a new invention may cause other firms to go out of business or even bring about the extinction of a whole industry. The defeated firms or industries are not assaulted or threatened; they just cease to get orders. But the extinction of a firm or an industry is not the same sort of thing as the extinction of an animal or a species. When the last are rendered extinct, particular animal organisms die and have no descendants. Physical death occurs. But the extinction of firms and industries does not necessarily involve the physical death of human organisms, even though a stockbroker may jump from the roof or handloom weavers die of hunger.[1] Bankruptcy may be described as economic death, but it is quite different from physical death. Firms themselves, indeed, may survive by changing the scope of their activities, and even if they are extinguished, the men who direct the work for them go elsewhere and work for other firms. Herbert Spencer's phrase 'the survival of the fittest' applies, therefore, to firms as well as to animals and animal species, but in its economic application it does not imply the physical death of those that fail to survive, but only the cessation of some groupings and activities and the assumption and organisation of new ones.

---

[1] The bankrupt stockbroker is generally 'hammered' and the employees of dying industries are nowadays retrained, redeployed or pensioned.

(b) Competition between suppliers of labour

We may now consider some moral implications of competition in the market for labour. When workmen compete with one another for jobs and firms compete with one another for workmen, wages vary in terms of its supply and of the demand for labour. It is well known that for several generations from the end of the eighteenth century employers in industrial countries had the upper hand over those who worked for them. The population was increasing, new industrial methods were making traditional skills useless to those who had them, and combinations among workmen were legally regarded as criminal conspiracies. Furthermore, the society within which the industrial revolution was taking place was already divided into classes and accustomed to the exercise of authority from above. In these circumstances workmen tended to be the losers in wage bargaining, and their situation was improved when legal obstacles to the formation of trade unions were removed, and improved still more when trade unions were given legal immunity from claims for damages.

Nowadays groups of employers negotiate with trade unions and in many industries no workman can get a job if he does not belong to a union, and may lose it if he does not strike when his union gives the order. Furthermore, it is a function of unions to prohibit unusually productive or efficient workmanship on the part of its members, and in this way competition between more efficient and less efficient workmen is prevented. Because of their need for votes, democratic political parties dare not seem to falter in advocating full employment. When there are more jobs than there are workmen to fill them, employers bid among one another for skilled men and in this way the total wages paid are often much higher than those negotiated between unions and employers' associations. At the same time there has been a growth of egalitarian sentiment, so that workmen are less inclined to fall in with their employers' wishes than they were in the nineteenth-century aftermath of aristocratic society.

(c) Competition between employers of labour

When there is full employment and unions bargain on behalf of men who have little fear of losing their jobs, there is competition between firms for the skilled labour they find it difficult to obtain, but little competition between workmen applying for jobs. If competition promotes efficiency, then the absence of competition among workers is likely to lessen their working efficiency. Trade unions, furthermore, tend to discourage speed and efficiency of work, and in so doing they tend to diminish pride in achievement and workmanship. In such conditions unions are not the protectors of the workers against grasping employers—the employers may *want* to grasp, but they just cannot do so—but aggressive fomenters of increased claims. If they did not act in this way they would not retain their members, since the terms of trade favour the workers in any case. The trade unions are thus tempted to require all workers to become union men and to regard themselves as united claimants from what the employers wilfully withhold from them. It is no longer a question of individuals competing for jobs as if they were prizes, but of the whole group extorting a collective prize for everyone. Bargaining comes into its own again, and the employers do well if they manage to settle for something less than the original demand. Instead of individuals competing with one another for scarce jobs, there are large organisations, manœuvring, compromising, bluffing and striking to secure collective transfers of wealth. Instead of competing with one another, the workers support organisations which threaten and fight for them.

Under conditions of full employment, then, employers compete for labour, even when they do not compete with one another in other ways. Employees, however, do not compete among themselves, but pay spokesmen to bargain for collective benefits on their behalf. It is not a situation of emulation and rivalry between individuals, but one of conflicting collectivities. But even in these conditions the *impersonal* competition I mentioned above still continues. As invention proceeds, for example, some industries decline by comparison with others. Thus oil and gas gain by comparison with coal, and road transport by comparison with the railways. Declining private industries may get state subsidies, declining nationalised industries may get both subsidies and other privileges. But unless they can be kept in being as museum pieces, like the Swiss Guards at the Vatican, they are reduced or eliminated

D

just like the unsuccessful firms in competitive market conditions. This competition is inseparable from the attempt to improve. Whenever someone tries to do something in a better way than it has been done before, others are faced with the choice of doing likewise or of being squeezed out. There may be no rivalry, no emulation, no struggle, no fighting, but just an exercise of originality or ingenuity by someone who has no intention of competing with or outdoing anyone.

(d) Competition to sell to consumers

We now come to competition to sell to ultimate consumers and the ethics of the relationships involved. There is a sense in which the ultimate consumers compete among themselves, in that a buyer who is unwilling to buy at the price that is asked may realise that there are others who will pay that price. The sellers, of course, compete with one another in providing what the consumers want at prices they will pay. The sellers also compete with one another in offering the consumers commodities they had not thought of before.

Competition between sellers is not unlike competition between firms for contracts and raises no new issues except those connected with advertising. Competition between buyers is hardly felt as such in competitive markets. This is because most consumers arrange their purchases according to their means, and go to those shops where the things they can afford are on sale. In societies divided into classes, few individuals think much about expenditures outside or beyond their ability to pay. But the situation is rather different when everyone thinks it possible or thinks it right that he should buy everything that is on offer. Then he may come to regard the rich man who pays high prices as competing against him, with superior buying power, for goods that he would like to have but is prevented from affording. When there is a single, classless market, the feeling of being, so to say, 'out-bought' by others is engendered. This encourages both demands for higher pay and demands for reductions in the spending-power of the richer consumers. I suggest that competition between consumers is not emulative when they think of their budgets in terms of their resources. It tends to become emulative when they take seriously the idea of expenditure beyond the limits of their present income. In the nineteenth century and earlier twentieth, those who had such ambitions aimed first to acquire the money necessary to satisfy them. They tried to get better paid jobs and they saved. But many consumers now hope for these results by collective measures exerted through trade unions and political parties. This is the reason why hopes and demands outrun resources and intensify the struggle for them. Whereas in the earlier forms of free competition individuals were encouraged to rely on their own efforts and abilities, in the system of cooperative conflict that has now emerged individuals hope to satisfy their desires by collective protection and pressure groups. The activities of individuals are merged into those of groups and masses.

Opponents of competitive markets often criticise the part played by advertisements in stimulating desire and demand. They assert that when competing firms advertise in order to encourage expenditure on their goods they stimulate a materialistic outlook and mould men's lives in doing so. It is true that advertisement can lead to increased sales,[1] but commercial advertisement is only part of the apparatus of persuasion that operates so massively in contemporary society. Ever since the eighteenth century political leaders have been saying that each individual has the right to pursue his happiness, and the results of this belief are being experienced in our day. The 'scramble' for consumption goods is due to the misleading belief that there is increased wealth to be had effortlessly for all rather than to economic competition. Individuals would be less willing to buy what advertisers tell them if they were more inclined to accept limitations on their desires. When, furthermore, governments encourage inflation, thrift becomes pointless except for those with very large incomes or very small outgoings or both. The inflation characteristic of our day results from the happiness-seeking moral outlook of our time as well as from clumsy attempts to apply Keynesian economic theories in democratic societies. Indeed, Keynes's economic theory was in part an expression of his opposition to the strenuous moralism of the Victorian era when it was generally considered right first to save and then to spend. This comes out in a passage of *The*

---

[1] Ralph Harris and Arthur Seldon, *Advertising in Action*, Hutchinson for the Institute of Economic Affairs, London, 1962.

General Theory of Employment, Interest and Money (Macmillan, 1936) where he writes, with reference to Mandeville's criticisms of the evils of saving:

No wonder that such wicked sentiments called down the opprobrium of two centuries of moralists and economists who felt much more virtuous in possession of their austere doctrine that no sound remedy was discoverable except in the utmost of thrift and economy both by the individual and the state. Petty's 'entertainments, magnificent shows, triumphal arches, etc.' gave place to the penny-wisdom of Gladstonian finance, and to a state system which 'could not afford' hospitals, open spaces, noble buildings, even the preservation of its ancient monuments, far less the splendours of music and the drama, all of which were consigned to the private charity or magnanimity of improvident individuals.[1]

In *The Fable of the Bees*, Mandeville called prodigality 'that noble sin', and elaborated this by saying: 'I mean the unmixed prodigality of heedless and voluptuous men, that being educated in plenty, abhor the vile thoughts of lucre.' Keynes, like his friend (and rival) Lytton Strachey, disliked the puritanism inculcated in Victorian times, and Mandeville's easygoing hedonism was congenial to him. It has now become congenial to large sections of the population and in doing so has served to increase both the effective demand for consumer goods and the belief that they ought to be available for the asking. It is in this moral climate that advertisers of consumer goods operate, and there will be a 'scramble' for them as long as this fundamental weather does not change. There is no consistency, and little honesty, in criticising competitive advertising and at the same time proclaiming the right of everyone to as much as they can enjoy.

Market commodities and non-market goods

In Chapter I (p. 6) I indicated that casualties of the competitive market system, those who are unable to maintain themselves by their own exertions, may need to be supported by non-market means. Children as such are hardly casualties, but, apart from family allowances and school tuition and meals, and medical care, they are supported by their parents, and, to a decreasing extent, incapacitated parents are supported by their children. Insurance is a means of dealing with casualties

---

[1] P. 362. Cf. the passage from the *Treatise on Money* (1930) quoted in Sir Roy Harrod's *The Life of John Maynard Keynes* (Macmillan, 1951), pp. 406–7, where the relation of thrift to enterprise and profit is most carefully stated. The anti-Victorian ambit of Keynes's outlook is made clear by Harrod in chapter 5 and elsewhere.

within the market mechanism itself, and in this way both firms and individuals may guard themselves against the effects of death, accident, illness and other human risks. If there are people who cannot afford to pay the premiums, and if there are misfortunes that the market cannot insure against, then casualties may have to be helped by other than market means to enter the market, except that the incapacitated may need personal care in kind.

It was because the market was thought incapable of helping people in need of help that poor relief, unemployment benefit and medical care was provided, by private charity, voluntary insurance or publicly financed agencies. Thus people get incomes they do not work for, to pay for food and clothing they could not otherwise buy. They also get subsidised lodging and 'free' medical treatment, although they might have money (or vouchers) to pay for them.[1] Sometimes, but rarely, the gratuitous benefits are forced from private individuals in what amounts to confiscation, as happens when the rents of private houses are controlled at uneconomic rates and the landlords in consequence have to house their tenants at their own expense. But for the most part, the casualties of the system receive help paid for by money collected in rates and taxes. As incomes rise the casualties become fewer because they can insure against sickness, accident, death and other uncertainties. When we say that the market cannot deal with the casualties of the system we are faced with the possibilities of voluntary private provision (charity), involuntary private provision (enforced gifts, as with some controlled rents), voluntary public provision (as with public appeals for victims of natural disasters), and involuntary public provision (as with taxation). It is the last that people generally have in mind when they speak of providing for needs outside the market.

We need not spend time considering the ethics of involuntary private provision. There is no morally defensible reason at all for forcing some individuals, irrespective of their incomes or circumstances, to give pecuniary help to beneficiaries whose incomes and circumstances have not been inquired into. In

---

[1] Ralph Harris and Arthur Seldon, *Choice in Welfare* (IEA, 1963 and 1965); A. T. Peacock and J. Wiseman, *Education for Democrats* (IEA, 1964); E. G. West, *Education and the State* (IEA, 1963).

this way benefits are provided for people who may not need them by people who may not be in a position to afford them. The public at large say that certain classes of people should be helped, and then take no steps to see that the help goes to those who need it or that it is provided by those who, in equity, should provide it. The existence of this system is a sign of moral abdication, and those who oppose its abolition can have no concern for justice.

For the charitable methods of helping the casualties of the market to be feasible there must be wealthy people and wealthy organisations, or there must be a widespread ability and willingness on the part of friends and neighbours to help their unfortunate fellows. In contemporary society families are so scattered and friendships are so dispersed, that less help comes from personal and family loyalties. Fewer people think they ought to help one another in these ways, although they are increasingly able to do so, and people in distress no longer expect to obtain much help this way. No doubt this unconcern has been encouraged by the establishment of public relief organisations, but whatever the reasons for it, the fact remains. When help is dispensed by charities and other organised bodies, enquiries may have to be made into the extent and nature of the need. But these bodies may not have the power to obtain the necessary information, and in any case their representatives may think that too close enquiry will destroy the charitable atmosphere. They may prefer to be deceived by some artful dodger rather than to probe too far into his affairs, and as a result honest need may pass unnoticed and unhelped. Furthermore, when the subservience of immediately post-aristocratic society diminishes, many of those in need have an aversion to receiving gifts of this sort. They know they have no *right* to gifts, and they think they do have a right to some other sort of assistance. Givers, even those giving to relieve distress, can give to whom they please. People in distress who are *not* relieved naturally come to think they are unjustly overlooked. Thus there arises the belief that those in distress have a right to receive assistance.

It is at this stage that it comes to be accepted that such assistance should be provided by monies raised through taxation. For if the indigent have a right to assistance, and if there is no one in particular against whom this right can be claimed, then it is the public at large who have to fulfil it. Agencies of the government can demand the information necessary to distribute assistance to those who need it in proportion to their need. In this way, the help is less subject to private whim and accident than private charity would be. Indeed, in large populations it might not be possible for charity to provide the necessary help on the requisite scale. In a democratic community the citizens are presumed to approve of the expenditure they pay their taxes to meet, and in general the presumption is well-founded.[1] The plight of the needy is brought to their attention and they do not wish to see them starved or rendered desperate.

But in housing, medicine and education the matter has been taken further than this. Let us take first the example of housing. At one time private bodies such as the Peabody Trust built blocks of flats to be let at cheap rents to those who could not afford unsubsidised accommodation. Local authorities then joined in and financed such accommodation by subsidies from the rates. Then the central government added to these subsidies and a position was reached in which a considerable proportion of the population live in publicly subsidised dwellings. In some areas, indeed, a majority of the population are so provided for. It then comes to be said that housing is and ought to be a 'social service' and should not be left to be bought and sold in markets. This might be put forward as part of an argument for a socialist system of society, but we are not now discussing it in that light. The arguments we are concerned with are (1) that when housing is scarce it should be distributed in accordance with need, just as food should be rationed in times of famine; and (2), that housing is something very special, in that without places to live in people cannot go about their other affairs. The assumption here is that some things are too fundamental and important for individual survival for them to be left to be settled by market decisions.

On the first of these two arguments, we need to know about the nature and causes of the scarcity before we decide that rationing of subsidised housing by officials is the only way out. Scarcity is a function of effective demand, and if large numbers

[1] Recent research suggests, however, that the public does not generally approve of indiscriminate 'universal' social benefits, Arthur Seldon, *Welfare and Taxation*, (IEA, 1968).

of people who cannot afford them nevertheless demand *new* houses, there are likely to be difficulties in supplying them. In general, the idea that everyone has a right to accommodation of the sort that he considers desirable is bound to lead to the idea and even to the creation of a shortage. Again, the legislation controlling rents has made it very unlikely that private companies will build houses to rent. Thus the legislation controlling rents has forced the provision of such houses on to the public sector. Once the local governments and central government agencies are organised for this purpose, interests are built up in our society which regard it as natural that they should expand and extend. These do not consist only of the officials and administrators, but also of the 'experts', that is to say, specialists who know about the organisation and statistics of the matter. Once local authorities have large housing departments, they regard extension of them as the most natural and effective way of dealing with housing shortages, and do not ask whether other measures could be taken which would lessen or remove the responsibilities of their departments. The combination of large organisations, interested 'experts' and lazy-minded good nature forms a public opinion that is unlikely to be critical.

It is the second argument, however, that takes us to the heart of the problem. If the most fundamental and important things must not be left to be supplied and bought in markets, then it is not housing alone that will be claimed as essentially a social service. Similar, indeed, more extensive claims, are made in respect of medical care and of education. There are at present no influential voices calling for the abolition of private house ownership, but there are many who say that no one should be allowed to buy or sell medical attention or education. Medical attention is a matter of life or death and education or the lack of it can make or mar a whole career. (Food or the lack of it is also a matter of life or death, but the nationalisation of food provision is not advocated on that ground.) Such important matters, it is said, should not be left to be settled by the purse, for if they are, the better-off will live longer, healthier lives and have better careers than the poorer members of the community.

Before we consider the moral issues involved in this attitude, it will be as well to notice a similarity between housing, medical care and education. In all three cases a large organisation has been first set up, 'experts' have collected around it, and what was first regarded as a rescue operation for some is now regarded as a right or perhaps even a necessity for all. Now that the National Health Service has been working for twenty years it is suggested that it is *morally wrong* for individuals to pay for medical care. The main argument used is that in so doing they divert to their own use medical skill which, if used in the National Health Service, would be used for people most in need rather than for those who can pay for it. What began as an organisation for ensuring that no one would go without medical care for lack of means may possibly turn into the only permitted source of such care. People would then be prevented from paying for better medical care. When, several years ago, doctors withdrew from the National Health Service in order to provide medical care for a group of paying patients, they were criticised on the ground that they were diminishing the amount of care available in the National Health Service and providing their paying patients with more than their due.

Similarly, the organised network of local authority schools is gradually ousting fee-paying schools, even though public education was first provided in order to ensure that parents should not escape their obligation to see that their children are educated. It is now being claimed that it is wrong for people to pay for education outside the public system. For in doing so, it is alleged, they are unfairly buying advantages and privileges for their children at the expense of those whose parents are less well-off. It appears that when the public bodies concerned with education and health grow very large, arguments are produced for swallowing up the remaining private concerns. Perhaps it is only because millions of people now own their houses and many children still hope to inherit from them that it is not likewise being argued that in buying a house for himself a man is 'jumping the queue' and obtaining unfair advantages for himself and his family.

An interesting example of the way in which this institutional imperialism works may be seen from the arguments devised in order to equate the relief of taxation allowed for interest payments on house mortgages with subsidies for council houses. The tax reliefs were granted at a time when house-ownership was being encouraged and when well-off people tended to buy houses for cash. Owing to inflation and high taxation it pays many more people than it used to to buy their houses by means of mortgages, and a good sum of money would be saved by the Treasury if this concession were withdrawn. Because of this, it is said that the wealthy are being subsidised in buying their houses just as the poor are subsidised by having houses at less than their economic rents. But the wealthy came to use this system of finance because inflation and high taxation made it financially advantageous for them to do so. Furthermore, if house-ownership were still regarded as a worthy object of public policy then it could be encouraged among the less well-off. As it is, the major effort is put into subsidised rented housing, and critics of this policy are then told that well-to-do house-buyers are also being subsidised. Yet it is public policy by way of inflation, high taxation and publicly provided housing that has made it appear that tax relief on house mortgages is a form of subsidy.

We must now consider the argument that some needs are so fundamental that their satisfaction should not be left to the market, but should be provided publicly. This amounts to saying that in what concerns their basic needs people should not be left to fend for themselves. Social reformers in the past have said that no one should be allowed to go without shelter, medical care and education of some kind. But now the view is that no one should be allowed to *buy* these things for himself, but should be allotted his fair share of them under a publicly organised scheme. Taxes would be paid in accordance with ability, and benefits allotted in accordance with need. In this way the communist rule 'from each according to his ability, to each according to his need', would be applied, not to economic activity, but to the sphere of welfare. Not to organise things this way would be to support injustice, privilege, discrimination.

My first comment is that this dual system of economic inequality and welfare equality contains within itself, to use Saint-Simon's expression, 'the seeds of its own destruction'. For few people, in the long run, are likely to work and contrive their utmost if they are to be in no better position, as regards the fundamentals of living, than the helpless, the lazy or the unlucky. The more egalitarian the welfare distribution, the less enthusiasm there is likely to be for the competitive economic activities that produce the wealth. Within the system of competitive capitalism the individual is supposed to do the best he can 'for himself', which generally means also for his family and any causes he has set his heart on. But if he is prevented from using his income or his profits for things that *he* wants, if he is forced to send his children to schools he does not like and to go to a doctor he does not trust, then he may well wonder whether his business activities are worth while. He would be discouraged still further if housing became entirely a matter of welfare, to be allocated only in accordance with need. Thus, the extension of welfare and so-called 'fair shares' from one field to another is not compatible with the system of competitive capitalism. Believers in capitalism who set no limits to the extension of the 'fair shares' principle are helping to stake out the ground in which their graves will be dug.

It will be said, however, that it is wrong to wish to buy privileges with superior wealth. We may now see the issue in this way: it is said by some that education and medical care are so important and fundamental that they ought not to be bought and sold, and by others that, just because they are so important and fundamental, they should be the responsibility of each individual. The conflict would appear to be between these two policies: (*a*) providing basic welfare at public expense and in accordance with need, and (*b*) each individual regarding himself as responsible for providing his own and his family's basic welfare according to his resources and his wishes.

Now it should be remarked in the first place that (*a*) is a much more cumbrous way of proceeding than (*b*). For under (*a*), the money has to be collected in taxes and used to pay for the doctors and hospitals to which the individual taxpayers then present themselves, whereas under (*b*) they pay the doctors and the hospitals direct. What reasons are put forward for preferring the roundabout way?

One reason is that it is a means of making the well-off pay towards the welfare of the poor. But this would only justify taxation to cover the welfare expenses of those who could not afford to pay for themselves. Yet what is being advocated is taxation to provide a service which is to be the *sole* service for everyone. Why, then, should those who can afford to, not pay for the welfare services they require for themselves and their families? Having contributed towards others, shouldn't they be free to look after themselves with what remains to them? Two reasons are given for answering these questions in the negative. The first is that if the better-off members of the community paid for private welfare services for themselves and their families, they would be enticing skill and other resources away from the state system and in this way lowering the level of the services it can provide. The second reason is that it is unjust that some people should have different and better welfare services than others, since welfare should be in accordance with need, not in accordance with ability to pay.

The first of these reasons is the less radical. It depends on the fact that a state system already exists, and is then put forward as the claim that nothing should be available outside it. It can be answered in the following way. Either only a few want services outside the state system, or many do. If only a few, then the effect on the whole system is small and there is no need to trouble about it. If many want services outside the system, this shows that many people can and do wish to be responsible for their own arrangements, even after they have been taxed to provide for others. Furthermore, the more people there are who wish for private provision, the fewer there are who need public provision. Again because they are paying for it themselves, those who opt out of the system are likely to employ existing resources more economically than do those who remain in the system.

Of course, it is the second, more radical reason that moves most of those who object to the buying and selling of medical care and education. They think it is unjust for people to spend money on schooling or medical care for themselves or their children, for in doing so they are buying privileges, and privileges should not be bought. If a privilege is merely an advantage, then the more intelligent and shrewder people are constantly buying privileges, since they constantly buy to better advantage than other people. If, however, a privilege is an *unjust* advantage, then to talk of buying privileges in these connections, is merely to assert that it is wrong to buy medical care or education.

50

Which things, then, is it right to buy and sell, and which things should be excluded from markets altogether? Professor R. M. Titmuss[1] thinks that human blood should not be bought and sold, but rather given and taken, and then only within the British National Health Service. Not many people object to the selling of human hair, although Kant thought the practice 'not entirely free from blame'.[2] All civilised peoples think it wrong to buy and sell human beings, yet these same societies regard the selling of one's labour, which is an activity of one's self even if not a part or organ, as morally acceptable. One can list some objects and activities which are universally regarded as morally unsuitable for purposes of buying and selling, e.g. votes, knowledge that would be useful to a foreign power, knowledge about a friend which would be of interest to a newspaper and its readers, sexual complaisance or sexual activity, a man's services as thief or killer. There are some things and activities which by their very nature *could* not be bought or sold. Love and tenderness, for example, presuppose a spontaneous concern on the part of the person who, as we say, *gives* them, and just could not be made available in return for a payment offered. On the other hand, care and attention can be bought, even though they can only be sold by someone who is conscientious and skilful.

However, we are not here concerned with any argument to the effect that medical care and education *cannot* be bought or sold, but with the argument that, like votes, knowledge acquired in friendship, and one's country's military secrets, they *should not* be. The last two are forms of betrayal and the first is bribery, and the relevant actions are wrong because betrayal and bribery are. Selling one's services as a thief or murderer are wrong

---

[1] In *Choice and 'The Welfare State'*, Fabian Tract No. 370, Feb. 1967, pp. 13–16. According to Professor Titmuss *sellers* of blood try to sell too much and so weaken themselves. Furthermore they tend to be 'Skid Row' characters and their blood is not always up to standard.

[2] *The Metaphysics of Morals* (1796) in *Werke* (Prussian Academy Edition) Vol. 6, p. 423. Kant thought that to 'give away or sell a tooth' or 'to submit oneself to castration in order to gain an easier livelihood as a singer' were somewhat akin to self-murder. Hair, as a *part* but not an *organ* of the body, was rather different, but even so, in selling it, an individual was treating a part of himself (and hence himself?) as a means rather than as an end in itself. Blood seems to be neither an organ nor a part of the body. In *The Price of Blood* (IEA, 1968), Michael H. Cooper and Anthony J. Culyer argue that 'payment, provided that it is separated from donation, would induce further supplies', and that 'payment for blood can be both sensible and humane' (p. 45).

because theft and murder are wrong, and prostitution is wrong because it denies human dignity on the part of both supplier and customer. Betrayal of a friend in the way mentioned above is not a *criminal* offence, but fidelity is not regarded as open to financial offers.

On the face of it, education and medical care are not, like treachery, bribery or theft, morally wrong or criminal and hence not rightly bought or sold for that reason. For many generations private doctoring and private schooling were not only tolerated, but were highly respected activities. Has anything happened, then, to change their moral quality? I suggest that it is the growth of the large state organisations connected with them that has led many people to change their moral attitudes towards them. When in the past a doctor set up in practice or a scholar opened a school, all he had to consider were his patients, pupils or colleagues. But nowadays the state educational and medical systems, and the 'experts' associated with them, join to accuse him of antisocial behaviour. It is not enough for him to help a number of particular individuals who pay him to do so, for, it is said, there are other individuals who need the help more, and in any case the people's representatives and the state apparatus they control know better than he does where doctoring and schooling can best be deployed. It is not the business of the law to interfere with a man's choice of a car, a diet,[1] or a form of sexual behaviour, but education and medical care are held to be quite different; inequality is permissible in the former, but not in the latter, because in the latter they are too important to be left to individual choice. Buying education is, indirectly, buying chances in life, and buying medical care is, in effect, buying life itself. The implication is that life chances ought all to be equal, that health and life should be equally considered through public authority, and that these equalities can in practice be achieved in these ways.

Now the critic of this outlook may deny that equality can be achieved in these ways. He may suggest that powerful people, politicians and their hangers-on prominent among them, would get advantages for themselves and their families which in

---

[1] Of course the state has a duty to require standards of food production and manufacture, since buyers are frequently unable to ascertain whether the food is poisonous, adulterated, etc. Similarly, the state justifiably requires school teachers, doctors, etc., to have certain qualifications.

the free system had been obtained by rich people. He may also suggest that sometimes those who pay for what they consider better things may be very much mistaken. But the main line of criticism, I suggest, ought to go to the implications of imposing an equality as regards education and health and of leaving individuals to pursue freely chosen lives in other ways. I have already suggested (pp. 48–9 above) that equalised welfare and a competitive economy are not likely to be able to exist together for very long. I now suggest that when they do live together their union is morally questionable. Broadly speaking, what is advocated is forcible communal and equalised provision of what is considered most fundamental to the individual, and freedom as regards the less fundamental, particularly the inessentials and luxuries. The government consider this to be 'getting our priorities right', since they see themselves organising the people so that they *receive* the fundamentals before they can concern themselves with anything else. The priorities are those of the government and presuppose that the government controls what people can do. But from the point of view of the individual the moral situation looks very different. Under the compulsory welfare system we are considering, schooling and medical care are organised in ways over which the individual has little control. They are not among the things that *he* has to work and save for—or so it seems to him, for the money for them is taken from him before he receives his pay. In the very process, there-fore, of being made *social* or *governmental* priorities, education and medical care cease to be *individual* priorities in the economy of the individual. As he is not allowed as an individual to spend money on these things, whatever sense of priorities he may have must be expressed in other directions. His responsibility in the spending of his money starts only after these fundamental services have been provided for him.

The consequences of publicly providing people gratis with services which would be of fundamental personal and moral importance if they had to provide them for themselves, are likely to be very far-reaching indeed. When the government imposes *its* priorities it alters the balance of the choices which the individual can make for himself. In the past it has been regarded as an individual's responsibility to direct his ex-penditure in the best possible way. This involved him in ensuring that he had dealt with essentials before he embarked on inessentials and luxuries. Some people made a better job of this than others, and there were, as we have emphasised, some whose mistakes or misfortunes made them casualties. But under the system we are now considering, no one is to be allowed to have personal control of his expenditure on some of the basic matters. But the more his needs are satisfied in this way, the more important will his expenditures on other things seem to him. Some of these other expenditures, such as those on food[1] and clothing, will be important enough, but luxuries and superfluities will play a large part among them. His sense of responsibility for what he is not allowed to decide for himself is likely to diminish, and it is possible that he will be less concerned for his health and his children's education than for his amusements. The very quality of his amusements, it may be suggested, varies in accordance with whether they are engaged in after he has himself provided for the fundamentals of his life, or whether they are the major part of the mere residue of personal choice allowed to him by a paternalistic society.

Let us consider the situation of a man who is not allowed to spend from his own income on his health or his children's education. Let us suppose, too, that his housing is subsidised and is of the standardised type usual for such accommodation. His control over the medical attention he and his family get, and over his children's schooling and his house is small. He can vote at national and local elections, and he can sometimes change his doctor or make protests about how the schools are organised. A man in this situation would give expression to his personal aims in spending the income he takes home from work after taxes have been deducted. Because his taxes are paid on his behalf by his employer, and because they finance what is publicly provided for him, his take-home pay appears to him to be his total pay. From this he has to buy food, clothing and furniture, but apart from such items it is amusements and luxuries that his 'wages' appear to buy for him. A likely consequence of this would be that the connection between work

---

[1] Diet is of great importance for individual health ('man ist was er isst', said Feuerbach), but no one proposes that diets should be publicly devised and imposed, even though bad diet must increase the calls upon the National Health Service. Subsidised school meals, however, have been defended on the ground that parents may fail to provide nourishing meals for their children.

and the provision of the state-provided fundamentals is obscured. The individual would be encouraged to believe that provision for such fundamentals as health and education is not his concern. When he presses for increased wages what he is likely to have in mind is the income he can spend as an individual, and he will probably think that the pre-empted taxation gets in the way of this. Unless he has strong religious convictions, or a concern for public work or for the exercise of some skill or artistic ability, he is likely to think that work is for food and amusement. Adam Smith said that 'it is perfectly self-evident' that 'consumption is the sole end and purpose of all production',[1] but to the inhabitant of a secularised Welfare State, it is amusement and luxury that are likely to appear as the main ends of production. For in such a society the system of taxation and of welfare expenditure conceals the connection between work and production on the one hand, and the consumption of welfare services on the other. We may call this the mystification of the Welfare State. If, on the other hand, people pay directly for their doctor and for their children's education, they are likely to approach the rest of their expenditure in a different and perhaps a more responsible manner.

Monopoly and cooperation

We have already discussed in the first section of this chapter, the idea that economic competition is a form of strife or rivalry and should therefore be morally condemned. We may now briefly consider the idea that competition is bad because it is opposed to cooperation which, as a form of harmony in human affairs, ought to be promoted as much as possible.

Deliberately organised cooperation is not, in itself, necessarily good. A cabal or gang may cooperate most amicably in carrying out an evil design, and hence the purpose for which the cooperators deliberately harmonise their actions and policies is relevant to the goodness or badness of what they are doing. Furthermore, people may cooperate without deliberately setting out to do so. This indeed is what generally happens when commodities are produced under competitive market conditions. In his *Harmonies Économiques*, Bastiat wrote of the

---

[1] *The Wealth of Nations*, Book 4, ch. 8.

mining, smelting, manufacturing, transporting, financing and storing involved in producing a cheap lamp for sale to a French workman. Firms and individuals all over the world had worked together in producing it, but no one man or body of men had organised all these processes so as to fit them together into a whole. There was detailed cooperation in hiring men, miners or metal-workers or dockers, buying materials, moving finished or semifinished products, and so on. But there was no single plan for lamp-manufacturing, organised from a single centre and requiring the acquiescence, obedience or enthusiasm of all the participants. The mineowner, the miner, the metalworker, the carrier, each pursued his own ends, and, without even considering the lamps that resulted, cooperated in producing them and getting them to the shops and to the purchasers. Competitive cooperation, therefore, is not a contradiction in terms, if we mean by it the working together that takes place without conscious participation in some comprehensive plan. There must, of course, be deliberate cooperation within firms, and between firms that contract with one another, but in a competitive economy the firms are not cooperating to execute a plan agreed between them all or imposed upon them.

Competition, then, is not opposed to cooperation, but rather to deliberate and comprehensively organised forms of it, as described, for example, by Engels in his *Fundamental Principles of Communism* (1847) in the words: 'When industry is conducted in common and in accordance with plans determined by the whole of society . . .'[1] Competition then, is not opposed to cooperation but is opposed to monopoly. There may be occasions when a monopoly is justified, as, for example, when the cost of producing a commodity is very much less when the total output is produced by one firm and there are substitutes to which consumers may turn if the price goes too high. But competition is not compatible with agreements between firms for limiting or eliminating it. On the practical effects of legislation to prevent monopoly, I am not competent to judge. But it should be emphasised that when there are substitutes for the monopolised commodity, and when it is open to new firms to come into the market, undesirable monopolies are not likely to persist. A competitive economy can put up with some monopolies and even publicly

[1] *Marx-Engels: Werke* (Dietz Verlag, Berlin, 1964), Vol. 4, p. 376.

organise some to its own advantage. It is when competition has already been seriously undermined that calls for anti-monopoly legislation are heard, and then it may be too late for them to be of much effect. Such may be the situation in Great Britain today.

IV. The Egalitarian Collectivist Alternative

Egalitarian collectivism and distributive justice

The form of collectivism we are now concerned with advocates help by the state for the casualties of the competitive system and the provision of basic welfare such as medical care, housing and education in accordance with need rather than in accordance with ability to pay. Two principles are relevant here. First there is the principle of a basic minimum, and second there is the principle that certain basic requirements and services should be distributed in accordance with need rather than in accordance with the financial resources of the recipient.

The liberal accepts the principle of a basic minimum without accepting the principle that medical care, education and the like should not be marketable goods. He argues that in a humane and wealthy society the poorest should not be left to suffer from illness and exposure and forced to remain without education in the basic skills. To help those in distress, he holds, and to respond to the call of humanity, is a moral demand that no one can reasonably question, but this response is concerned with relieving suffering, not with achieving justice. It is one thing, he argues, to bring help in order to relieve suffering, and quite another to bring help in order to achieve justice. The first does not necessarily lead in an egalitarian direction whereas the second tends to do so. If the poor or the casualties of life are helped because it is *unjust* that they should remain as they are, then the way is opened for saying that it is unjust that some people should be less well-off than others. But if the help given to them is given on *humanitarian* grounds, then there is no presumption in favour of continuing the process of redistribution beyond the point at which distress is relieved. Of course, what constitutes distress will vary to some extent with the level of wealth of the community. But this is a very different thing from saying that everyone should be equally well-off.

58

The collectivist we are now considering, then, is concerned at the injustice of inequality as well as by the distress of the needy. Wealth, he argues, gives its possessors advantages which it is unjust that they should have. Basic needs, he believes, should be satisfied in accordance with their urgency, not in accordance with the financial resources of those who have them. Thus while everyone believes that suffering calls for relief, the egalitarian collectivist claims that inequality calls for remedial redistribution.

Distributive justice and commutative justice

The philosophical discussion of justice started with Aristotle's account of the matter in Book V of his *Nicomachean Ethics*. Here Aristotle distinguished between distributive justice on the one hand and corrective or remedial justice on the other. He also appeared to have in mind a form of justice which has since been called catallactic or commutative justice, and there has been discussion whether this is a species of corrective or remedial justice or a distinct kind. In his *Aristotle*[1] Sir David Ross writes of three forms of justice, the third of which he calls 'commercial'.

By distributive justice Aristotle meant justice in the distribution of such things as property, honour or bodily safety. In his view, a distribution was just when the goods (or evils) distributed were distributed equally or fairly, and they were distributed equally or fairly when they were distributed according to merit. By 'merit' Aristotle did not mean a person's individual moral worth, but rather his just claims on the basis of status or contributions to the society. Aristotle appears to have been thinking of the distribution of profits in accordance with shares in a business and of the distribution of some public gain by an authority with the right to allocate it. By 'distributive justice' he therefore meant distribution in accordance with the rightful claims of the parties to and between whom the distribution was to be made. We may illustrate one aspect of his view of distributive justice by considering how prize money used to be distributed in the British Navy, when each individual received his share of the prize in accordance with his rank, the admiral receiving a large sum, the captains a smaller share, and so on.

[1] W. D. Ross, *Aristotle* (1st edn, Methuen, 1923), p. 212.

By corrective justice on the other hand, Aristotle meant the form in which a party has a right to redress against another party, either because one of the parties has failed to fulfil a contract, or because one of the parties has injured the other. In such cases justice is secured when the situation has been adjusted or put right, by obtaining fulfilment of the contract or payment in lieu of that, or by payment of damages in the case of assault.

Aristotle's view of catallactic justice, or justice in exchange, appears to be that justice is secured when the producers of the goods exchanged receive payment in proportion to the real value of what is produced or the merit of the producers. Aristotle's meaning is not clear, but he appears to assume that, although demand is what gives rise to exchange value, and although money is a means of facilitating exchange, there is some natural or just relationship of value between the various types of manufactured goods, such that, to use his examples, a bed or a house is really worth so many pairs of shoes.

St Thomas Aquinas took over Aristotle's general account of justice, interpreting it in his own orderly manner. He retained Aristotle's adjective 'distributive' for the one form of justice, but introduced the word 'commutative' for the other, arguing that justice in exchange is a form of commutative justice in which goods are bought and sold at prices which reflect their real values. In his *Commentary on Aristotle's Ethics* St Thomas says that an exchange is just when there is a just reciprocity (*juste contrapassum*). Before we pass on to consider later views, we must call attention to some important features of the Aristotelian–Thomist analysis of justice.

First, it must be emphasised that both Aristotle and St Thomas thought of distributive justice in terms of the distribution of some public gain or windfall among citizens or members of a partnership. They both recognised that this has to be done by some authority in the light of the merits or claims of the parties between whom the distribution is being made. They both took it for granted that this was happening in a society in which there was an established order and system of property. Neither of them had in mind the reform of society by means of a redistribution of goods and services in terms of some ideal system of social justice.

Second, Aristotle and St Thomas thought that there was a just price at which goods should be sold and that this was a price that reflected the 'real' value of the goods. They thought that as food is to shoes, or as farmers are to leather workers, so the relative prices of food and shoes should be. It followed that they regarded prices as matters of justice and hence of morality. If what I said in Chapter II above is correct, then they were wrong in believing this. Injustice occurs in a trade transaction when a party does not fulfil his contract, and the injustice is corrected when he is made to do so or to pay compensation. But in competitive markets prices are settled by supply and demand, and no price is just or unjust as long as buyers and sellers are honest with one another. If 'just price' means anything, it means only the price that the buyer and seller have agreed. The analysis of justice began to be wrongly stated when Aristotle included justice in exchange as a form of justice, and it went still further awry when St Thomas used the word 'commutative' to mean both what Aristotle called remedial justice and the supposed just price in the exchange of goods.

Third, it should be noticed that authorities play a different part in distributive justice from the part they play in exchange transactions. The distribution is *made* by an authority. If there were no authority to make it, there could be no distribution, just or unjust. On the other hand, individuals exchange goods between one another; it is they who determine who gets what, not some authority over them. Government is needed, of course, to prevent violence and fraud, but the government is not a party to the exchanges. It sees that the agreements are not broken with impunity, but it does not make them. It is natural, therefore, to use the term commutative justice to mean just dealing between individuals, and just dealing between individuals is dealing in which agreements are freely made and honestly kept. Distributive justice is exercised by an authority, commutative justice by and between individuals.

We may now consider distributive justice in more general terms. It is the distribution of goods or services or burdens (as with taxation or military service) in accordance with some rule. According to Aristotle, this means distribution in accordance with merit, but by 'merit' he appears to mean something like 'just claims', and this does not take us very far. Professor

Chaim Perelman in *The Idea of Justice and the Problem of Argument*[1] mentions the following types of rule that have been considered distributively just: the same to everyone, i.e. equal distribution; to each according to his merits (moral merit?); to each according to his works; to each according to his needs; to each according to his rank; to each according to his legal entitlement. Professor Nicholas Rescher in *Distributive Justice*[2] does not list the rule of rank, but amplifies the rule of merit with the phrase 'ability or merit or achievements', and adds further rules, one of which is 'according to their efforts and sacrifices' and the other 'according to a valuation of their socially useful services in terms of their scarcity in the essentially economic terms of supply and demand'. (p. 73).

This last is not a rule of distributive justice at all. For distributive justice involves an authority who makes the distribution in accordance with a rule, but in competitive markets individuals exchange goods with one another and their gains or losses are not *allocated* to them by anyone, but accrue according to their luck or perspicacity. There is no need for any authority to distribute in accordance with scarcity and supply and demand, for that happens anyway in a competitive market. To say that such a distribution is distributively just is to suppose an authority where there is none. To say that such a distribution is commutatively just is merely to say that no one has used force or fraud.

Through competitive markets, opportunities, incomes and wealth come to people according as they are lucky, clever, industrious, or have some rare ability that is in demand. Doctors (once established in a practice) earn more than filing clerks, school teachers less than air pilots. Businessmen may hope to make fortunes, poets can reasonably hope only to have their works read and admired. No one has *decreed* these things, for they are the unplanned consequences of history, convention, chance, relative scarcity and many other things besides. There is no one who distributes things in this way, no one who says that doctors should get so much and teachers so much less, no one who makes poets seek for jobs in a bank rather than hope

[1] C. Perelman, *The Idea of Justice and the Problem of Argument* (Routledge, 1963).
[2] N. Rescher, *Distributive Justice* (New York, Bobbs-Merrill, 1966). This book contains a comprehensive bibliography.

to earn a living from their poetry. These incomes come about as a result of all sorts of particular bargains, acquiescences, resistances, windfalls and expectations.

Is what emerges in this way just or unjust? I suggest that the question, as generally put, is a confused one. If the doctor's client cheats him, if the teacher fails to keep up to date in his knowledge, if the businessman fails to deliver what he has promised, then breaches of commutative justice have taken place. But what is just or unjust about the whole situation in which they find themselves? If no one is responsible for bringing it about, no one can reasonably be commended for arranging it justly or blamed for arranging it unjustly. The rain that falls upon the just and upon the unjust cannot be condemned for its lack of concern for moral distinctions. Neither can a social order be condemned as unjust if no one has planned and controlled it. If a whole system of social and economic relationships is held to be unjust, this must really mean that *if* someone had made the distribution deliberately, *then* it would have been unjust. But something that merely *happens* can be neither just nor unjust. It is not unjust for a good man to die in an accident and for a bad man to live long and happily.

When, therefore, the socialist says that it is unjust for opportunity and wealth to depend largely on luck and birth he is implying that they *should be* deliberately distributed in accordance with some rule or standard.[1] This *follows* from his wish to establish justice in society as a whole. Distributive justice implies a distributor, such as a judge, teacher or parent, who acts in accordance with some rule of distribution. He intervenes to bring something about that would not otherwise have happened. In a world in which wealth and opportunity are not the same for everyone all sorts of inequalities arise and tend to be accentuated. To introduce distributive justice into it, some man or body of men must alter it in terms of a system of rules. The differences between the incomes of doctors and air pilots and filing clerks and poets must be settled in accordance

[1] It is significant that when Henry Sidgwick discusses the socialist distribution of wealth he compares it with Divine Justice, secured by the will of the Deity. 'If the Socialistic Ideal . . . could be realised without counter-balancing evils, it would certainly seem to give a nearer approximation to what we conceive as Divine Justice than the present state of society affords' (*The Methods of Ethics*, (7th edn, Macmillan, 1907), 1930 reprint, p. 289). God is not only the Creator of the world, but its supreme lawgiver and regulator.

with principles of justice. Known and accepted rules must be followed by those who re-model the social order. There must be some governmental organisation which, like Mr Aubrey Jones and his Prices and Incomes Board, combines the functions of judge, teacher and parent, and the population must accept their authority. In seeking for distributive justice in the community as a whole in addition to distributive justice in families and firms, egalitarian collectivists require there to be some public father or non-commercial board of directors to arrange the distribution.

Before passing on to the next section, I should like to consider Professor John Rawls's views on justice in general and on distributive justice in particular, since his treatment of these topics cannot be ignored in any contemporary discussion of justice in society. According to Rawls, the notion of fairness is fundamental to that of justice.[1] He asks his readers to imagine a number of free and rational individuals considering, before its formation, what rules and institutions they should give to the society they are about to form. We imagine them, that is, in process of entering into a social contract. In order that they shall not be tempted by considerations of their own personal interest, they must be supposed ignorant both of their own past position, and of their own powers and abilities. Nevertheless, they must be supposed to have actual or potential family ties and a regard for such things as religious truth. These individuals would, if rational, choose a set of institutions of such a nature that they would not mind if their enemy decided the place they were to occupy in it. For with families and other interests at stake, and in ignorance of their own prospects of success or failure, they would opt for institutions that would not be atrociously hard on anybody. They would, in consequence, come to accept two principles of justice. According to the first, each person involved in the institution of the society would have to have an equal right to as much freedom as is compatible with a like freedom for the others. According to the second, the institutions set up should be such as to be to everyone's advantage, and the offices in them should be open to all. A basic idea here is that of reciprocity. The contracting parties would

---

[1] 'Justice as Fairness', in *Philosophy, Politics and Society*, ed. P. Laslett and W. G. Runciman, Series II (Oxford, Blackwell, 1962).

try to set up a system in which no one is assigned a purely sacrificial role. This, in brief, is Rawls's account of justice in general.

Distributive justice, he holds, is concerned with the inequalities in income and wealth, and in social prestige and status, required in order to fulfil the two principles mentioned above. It is the second principle of justice that is most important here. A system of inequalities in wealth and income can only be justifiable if it is in the interest of a representative member of the general body of people. This would mean that the amount of inequality that is permissible would be the amount necessary to provide incentives for entrepreneurs so to conduct trade and industry that increases in wealth would accrue even to the least advantaged. Those who are favoured by nature would be enabled to gain only on terms that would also improve the wellbeing of the least endowed.

Thus, we suppose that, in addition to maintaining the usual social overhead capital, government provides for equal educational opportunities for all either by subsidising private schools or by operating a public school system. It also enforces and underwrites equality of opportunity in commercial ventures and in the free choice of occupation. This result is achieved by policing business behaviour and by preventing the establishment of barriers and restrictions to the desirable positions and markets. Lastly, there is a guarantee of a social minimum which the government meets by family allowances and special payments in times of unemployment, or by a negative income tax.[1]

This idea of a minimum is very important. Clearly, the contracting individuals described by Rawls will have possible misfortune in view, and will wish to ensure that if misfortune is to be their lot, it will be as bearable as possible. This leads Rawls to consider how the proportion of the society's resources that ought to be allocated for savings could be fairly decided. An extra factor here is the fairness of imposing savings on one generation for the benefit of future generations. On Rawls's view, this means that the contracting parties choose as if they did not know to which generation they belong.

The saving of those worse off is undertaken by accepting, as a matter of political judgment, those policies designed to improve the standard of life,

---

[1] 'Distributive Justice', in *Philosophy, Politics and Society*, Series III (Oxford, Blackwell, 1967), p. 69.

thereby abstaining from the immediate advantages which are available to them. By supporting these arrangements and policies the appropriate savings can be made, and no representative man regardless of generation can complain of another for not doing his part.[1]

Saving for what Rawls calls 'various grand projects' would not necessarily coincide with saving justly. He concludes his main discussion as follows:

This account of distributive shares is simply an elaboration of the familiar idea that economic rewards will be just once a perfectly competitive price system is organised as a fair game. But in order to do this we have to begin with the choice of a social system as a whole, for the basic structure of the entire arrangement must be just. The economy must be surrounded with the appropriate framework of institutions, since even a perfectly efficient price system has no tendency to determine just distributive shares when left to itself.[2]

In an article entitled 'Justice and Fairness',[3] Professor John W. Chapman criticises Rawls's first account of his view, that is, his account of justice as fairness prior to his later account of distributive justice. Chapman argues that Rawls's account of justice, by placing fairness and reciprocity at the centre of it, fails to take account of rights and of needs. As to the former, Chapman points out that on Rawls's view the contracting parties might agree to the institution of slavery. Rawls accepts this consequence, but in doing so has in mind a society in which military victors have the right to kill the conquered. As to the latter, Chapman considers that justice as fairness cannot deal with the idea that it is just that certain basic needs should be satisfied even if the person in need makes no contribution to the society. I should say here that help given in such circumstances is given not on grounds of justice but of humanity. Rawls's discussion of justice in saving seems as if it may have been written with Chapman's paper in mind, for the level at which unfortunates can be maintained depends upon the productivity of the society and upon the general willingness of its members to forgo immediate consumption for themselves.

With Rawls's central theme that fairness and reciprocity are central to justice I agree, although I have taken my terminology from the Aristotelian–Thomist tradition and have drawn

---

[1] *Ibid.*, pp. 75–6.   [2] *Ibid.*, pp. 78–9.
[3] In *Justice: Nomos VI*, ed. Carl J. Friedrich and John W. Chapman (New York, Prentice-Hall, 1963).

conclusions with which Rawls might not agree. A point I notice in his 'Distributive Justice' is that at the beginning he lists as items to be distributed, incomes and wealth, and social prestige and status, and yet in the body of his article he discusses only the first two. Perhaps he was right not to deal with the second two ideas, for they not only differ between themselves —prestige is more general and more informally awarded than status is—but they both also differ from wealth and income. Wealth and income can be increased in total amount and spread more or less equally. Wealthy people might become more wealthy at the same time as poor people become less poor. But it is not so clear that everyone's status could be increased in this way, for an improvement in status for those who, if the expression be allowed, have less of it, is likely to be obtained at the expense of those with more. Status is concerned with how people regard one another, the respect or deference they accord to one another, and this seems to belong to the region of recognition, of pride and respect, rather than to that of justice.

   We have seen that Rawls emphasises the importance of equality of opportunity for securing justice. Education, on his view, is to play a part in this by subsidies for private schools or by operating a state system. It will be noticed that he does not regard publicly provided education as the only method of working towards equality of opportunity. It seems important, however, to look more closely at what equality of opportunity implies. We may speak of *making* opportunities, of *taking* opportunities, and of *being given* opportunities or of *being presented with* them. Is equality of opportunity the equal chance of making opportunities for oneself? This would appear to assume an energy and intelligence that few people have, so that it would be straining the expression to use it only for the freedom to make opportunities for oneself. On the other hand, it would be straining the expression the other way if it were taken to mean that everyone is to have opportunities lying, so to say, ready to hand, requiring little or no trouble to be utilised. Indeed, this is hardly possible, since any individual can fail to utilise or to take an opportunity offered to him. I suggest, therefore, that *taking* opportunities is central to the very concept of equality of opportunity, which in consequence presupposes a certain spontaneity and activity on the part of the taker. If this is so, we may expect that those who wish to equalise opportunities for everyone in the sense of placing opportunities before them within government-organised educational systems, will find that only a proportion of those to whom this is offered will accept the offer. The equalisers are then tempted to put more and more emphasis upon *giving* and *presenting* and this is likely to involve placing hindrances in the way of the makers and the takers. This means that a policy that began as an attempt to increase freedom turns back upon itself and imposes monopolistic prohibitions. This is how state education in some Western countries, not least Britain, has developed.

Distributive justice in the satisfaction of needs

The establishment of distributive justice, then, as between all the members of a democratic state, would require a government that decided what each type of citizen and worker ought to receive, and a population that was in general agreement with the government on what the principles of distribution should be. The difficulties in the way of establishing acceptable principles of distribution are well known. Should distribution of income be in terms of merit, effort, output, or, if in terms of some or all of these, what system of weighting should be used? These questions are so difficult that most collectivists nowadays have given up the attempt to answer them and concern themselves chiefly with the distribution of basic needs such as health, housing and education. In this realm they consider the principle of distribution to be the fairly simple one of requiring that each individual should receive in terms of his *needs*. For a distribution to be made there has to be a distributor, and this, in the case we are considering, is to be the democratically elected government. It is assumed, for example, that it is easier to ascertain that a doctor needs such and such an education and that a filing clerk needs such and such a different education, than to decide what the doctor's salary should be in comparison with that of the filing clerk.

But the question that then has to be decided is: who is to be trained to be a doctor and who is to be trained to be a filing clerk? Those, it would seem, who have the necessary desire and aptitudes for the jobs in question. How, then, are the aptitudes to be ascertained? In the collectivist scheme of things aptitudes would be ascertained in the light of progress through the comprehensive schools which egalitarians favour. In Britain, the great majority of posts available for medical men are in the National Health Service, and the training given to fill them is financed by the state. If, as is the case, more people want to become doctors than there are opportunities for training, those who get into the medical schools do so as a result of *competition*, which is no different from the so-called 'rat-race'[1] that takes place in the schools. If, again, medical care is distributed by the state, then the number of those who can receive medical training depends on the number that the National Health Service employs. Does this number depend on *need*? There is no doubt that in this country many more doctors would be employed if *the wishes* of the population for medical attention could settle the matter. But this number would be much larger than could be met by the financial and physical resources likely to be allocated for it by the state out of taxation. As patients, people want more medical care than they wish to pay for as taxpayers. The egalitarian view is that this scarce care should be distributed in accordance with need.

It is clear, however, that 'need' is and will be interpreted in more than one way. The individual *to whom* the distribution is made does not always have the same conception of need as the individual *by whom* the distribution is made. The recipient tends to interpret it in terms of what he wants. If he wants a medical examination, for example, that is what he 'needs'. The distributor, on the other hand, is more likely to distinguish between what the recipient thinks he needs and what in the distributor's opinion he really needs, and to wish to make his distribution in terms of the latter. If everything that anybody wanted could be supplied to him, then distributive justice would be unnecessary. It is because not all wants can be supplied that some rule of

---

[1] What is this 'rat-race'? In the course of their school careers children exhibit aptitudes, talents and ambitions of various sorts in varying degrees. By some means or other those who can and want to undertake the most exacting types of work that require long training must be distinguished from the rest. An attempt to give this training to children who do not want or cannot complete it must lead to misery and waste of effort. If all were capable of undertaking it, only some could be selected to do so. Selection of some sort is unavoidable and the expression 'rat-race' serves only to vituperate the inevitable.

distribution, some 'rationing' has to be established. Needs, then, are generally held to be wants that are in some sense basic, wants the non-fulfilment of which destroys or severely hurts the individual who has them. Distribution of medical care, then, in accordance with need, would be distribution of it to those who would die or suffer serious harm if they received no care, and distribution among the members of this category in accordance with the degree of their possible loss or injury.

The type of health service, however, which egalitarians support, is one to which everyone belongs and from which everyone can claim medical attention, without fee, for slight as well as for serious illnesses. Everyone, then, is to receive in accordance with his wish, want or basic want, in accordance with his whim or in accordance with his dire need. Since the resources for supplying medical services are limited, it can be said that in general there is competition for these services between all those entitled to them, so that the mildly ill compete with the desperately ill. This is to some extent concealed because not *everyone* competes for the services of the brain surgeon or the 'heart-machine'. But the services of nurses and non-specialist doctors are, so to say, *diluted* between those who are seriously ill and those who are hardly ill at all. The patient with a cold takes up time and expense that might have been employed in giving a more thorough diagnosis to someone else. Furthermore, in a comprehensive scheme of this sort, the selfish, the demanding and the well-connected can gain attention at the expense of others.

In an egalitarian scheme, therefore, in which everyone can gain some attention on demand and without fee, the services given are likely to be diluted, the givers of the services are likely to be overworked, and the most selfish are likely to get attention at the expense of the more conscientious or amiable members of the community. When some quarrelsome individual enters a group he causes disputes and perhaps violence even though the other members of the group are pacific. The desire of the others for peace cannot preserve peace if there are a few who do not want it. It is somewhat similar, I suggest, with unreasonable or unnecessary demands on a public service. If a few individuals start to push their claims too high, others are induced to make similar claims to ensure their 'stake' in the available resources. There is something rather like Gresham's Law, and irresponsible behaviour tends to drive out responsible behaviour. The egalitarian collectivist, therefore, in removing the competition that arises from cash demand, substitutes for it competition by means of entreaty or bullying. It is nowadays regarded as rather indecent to refer to the abuses to which collectivist schemes are liable. The suggestion is that the critics of such abuses are self-righteous and show a contempt for the poor. But in a collectivist system such as the National Health Service to which practically everyone belongs irrespective of his income, some of the well-to-do are likely to be much more effective in obtaining special benefits than the less articulate among the poor.

The conclusion I draw from this is that basic welfare should not be removed from the market and provided for everyone out of taxation. Poverty and misfortune are evils but are not injustices, and the moral demand they make is for help on the ground of humanity. In matters as basic in their lives as health, housing and the education of their children it is best for people to allocate their own resources as far as they can, with public provision (when possible as purchasing power) in reserve for what they cannot individually pay for. If they are not allowed so to provide for themselves out of their disposable income they will come to regard their basic requirements as somebody else's business and to regard amusement as the chief aim of their free choices.

This is a convenient point at which to consider briefly the position of those well-off people who favour the enforced universality of publicly provided health and educational services, but meanwhile pay for private treatment in hospital for themselves and private schooling for their children. They can defend this *Interimsethik* by saying they are justified in so behaving while they support the coming of a system in which money can no longer buy such advantages. Their assumption is that individuals are morally justified in taking full advantage of privileges they believe they ought not to have as long as they support their eventual abolition. Whether they would consider a vote at an election as sufficient to constitute support I do not know, but, leaving this aside, it appears that they must believe that it is right for them to do what they consider wrong as long

F

as other people who do not think it wrong are not legally prohibited from doing it. They will not act on their principles unless other people are prohibited from acting on theirs.

They may argue, of course, that if they were to refuse to take advantage of what they consider to be unfair privileges others, with different views, would go on benefiting from them, and their own principled actions would have no tendency to alter the system. This may seem rather like the individual in the State of Nature depicted by Hobbes who will not refrain from aggression on others until there is a power capable of coercing *everyone* to keep the peace. There is an important difference, however, between the position of the wealthy egalitarian 'queue jumper' and the apprehensive natural man who longs for peace, but is reluctant to give away his advantages meanwhile. For everyone may be supposed to wish for self-preservation and the peace that fosters it, whereas large numbers of people see no harm in paying for extra services for themselves and their children, especially if they have earned the money to do so. To refuse to act on a moral principle unless and until everyone is forced to observe it, irrespective of their moral beliefs, is a strange way of showing one's adherence to it. It seems to me that someone who takes this view would feel justified in taking personal advantage of whatever new system was set up. Once fee-paying schools were abolished, for example, the wealthy could congregate in districts where there are particularly good schools and hospitals, arguing that they are justified in doing this as long as the good teachers and doctors have not been forcibly spread equally all over the country, or as long as a 'busing' system for children and patients has not been instituted. The stress all the time is on the system, and the individual considers himself free to try to beat it whenever he can, and more particularly whenever it is not perfect, which, of course it will never be. Yet no system can work well unless individuals are prepared to govern their *own* actions by principle irrespectively of what others do.

Two collectivist objections considered

There are two main objections to the view summarised on the previous page. The first is that if left to themselves people will not provide these things for themselves even if they have the wherewithal to do so. It is hard to know what to say in reply to this argument, which seems to assume that problem families are typical of the community as a whole. A forcibly imposed system of universal welfare might *make* people become like this, but it is premature to suggest that the transformation has already taken place. Dr E. G. West has shown[1] that before the Education Act of 1870 most parents were proud to make personal payments towards the education of their children. But that was over a hundred years ago and perhaps presentday parents, it may be objected, are no longer like that. Ralph Harris and Arthur Seldon[2] have ascertained that many people nowadays would *like* to make their own choices about welfare and pay more for them rather than rely wholly upon what the state provides. The remarkable thing is that such eminently responsible individuals are criticised by egalitarians as 'queue jumpers' if they so express themselves. One cannot help suspecting that egalitarians think there is something morally evil in the desire to foster the development of one's own children, to look after one's own health and to own one's own house, even in a society where minimum standards are at a level undreamed of by the pioneers of the welfare state.

This brings us to the second objection to the idea that in an economically advanced community individuals should be free to make and pay for their own choice of welfare. Dr Brian Barry[3] has argued with force and subtlety against some of the socialist arguments in favour of confining medical care and education to the publicly provided system. Nevertheless he appears to favour this course on other grounds—'because one places value on integration as such'. We may note, he says, that from the point of view of integration 'every departure from a complete ban on private provision must be regarded as a concession.'[4] He also suggests that integration is bound up with democracy in the following way:

As far as each parent determining the education of his child is concerned private schools offer as much scope as public in principle since private

[1] *Education and the State* (IEA, 1965), see esp. pp. 140–4 and 171.
[2] *Choice in Welfare 1965: Second Report on Knowledge and Preference in Education, Health Services and Pensions* (IEA, 1965).
[3] *Political Argument* (Routledge, 1965), ch. 7.   [4] *Ibid.*, p. 132.

schools may be run by the parents of the children attending them. But if
what one values is that the members of the community should determine as
one group how the next generation is to be educated, there is no substitute
for public schools.[1]

The emphasis here is upon the *oneness* of the group that deter-
mines how the next generation shall be educated. Dr Barry
does not notice, however, that the one group will also be
treating the next generation as one, so that parents and non-parents
of one generation will be imposing a uniform mode of education
on the next. He does not, nevertheless, regard integration as a
very strong value, even though he does consider it essential to
some collectivist arguments, and he puts forward three other
arguments for eliminating private choice in welfare. He argues
that a society with a variety of methods for providing welfare 'is
liable to serious splits to heal which there will be no shared
experiences and standards'.[2] Furthermore, in such a society
there will be inefficiency, because wealth rather than ability
will secure entry to positions of power. And finally he asserts
that in an integrated system of welfare, the powerful would have
a strong motive for improving the forms of welfare that are
publicly provided, since they themselves would have to use
them and would therefore want them to be as good as
possible.

This last argument has been implicitly met by Professor
Hayek[3] in *The Constitution of Liberty*. He points out that in a
society where the free market has scope, the better-off tend to
pioneer various types of consumption which are then made
available for larger sections of the population. The same
principle, I suggest applies to welfare, especially to education
where private schools have set standards and carried out
experiments which the publicly provided schools have then
made beneficial use of. As to Dr Barry's second argument, it
seems to me that a free market economy is less prone to
hierarchy than is the bureaucratic sort of society that socialism
requires. This topic will be discussed later. As to the alleged
'divisive' effects of a society which permits free choice in welfare,

[1] By 'public schools' Dr Barry means, of course, schools provided without fee out
of taxation.
[2] *Political Argument*, p. 134.
[3] F. A. Hayek, *The Constitution of Liberty* (Routledge, 1960), pp. 42–6.

one is back with 'integration' once more. Societies such as those in France, the United States and Great Britain contain all sorts of institutions, traditions of thought and action, regional idiosyncrasies and cultural oppositions. The distinctions between Catholics and free thinkers, between North and South, between England and Scotland have sometimes led to violence and are continual sources of strain. But if they were all eliminated the nations within which they exist would lose much of their energy and creative power. The suggestion that the people of these countries would be made better by forcing them all to go to the same schools and the same doctors in organisations administered by bureaucrats under the sort of control that democratic government permits is incredible in itself and dangerous because of the disappointment its realisation would give rise to.[1] I have already argued that under such a system individual effort would be guided by trivial aims because individuals would be prevented from directing their energies on the things that concern them most.

In a beautifully argued letter to the *Spectator*[2] Antony Jay indicates that if, as the Royal Commission on the Public Schools assumed, it is 'divisive' for parents to pay for their children to go to public schools, it is equally 'divisive' if some people are allowed to operate private cars when a public transport system exists. Owners of private cars, for example, 'can use their wealth to buy access to parts of the country which are denied to their fellow citizens who, through no fault of their own, have to rely on the state transport system'. If everyone, including Cabinet Ministers, had to make use of the public transport system, there would be more pressure on it to improve, and furthermore, by being forced to use public transport people would get 'enriching experience' and be saved from 'the arrogant isolation and social privilege of the private car'. The majority on the Commission on Public Schools wanted half the places at them to be used for children 'in need' of such education. Mr Jay suggests that places in those private cars that remained in a society where public transport predominated could be allocated to 'those suffering from infectious and

[1] It is possible that such disappointment is one reason for the bad temper and violence that are so widespread in Great Britain in the late nineteen-sixties and early seventies.
[2] 2 August 1968.

contagious diseases, halitosis, agoraphobia and diseases of the central nervous system'.

Collectivist organisation

As soon as the shape of modern society began to become apparent a distinction was drawn by students of it between forms of organisation in which uniformity was obtained by means of force and societies in which harmonious development is obtained by means of freely made agreements. In 1817 in *L'Industrie*[1] Saint-Simon distinguished between military and industrial forms of society. The military form, he held, was obsolete and its decline was made inevitable by the French Revolution. The old military and landed aristocracy was being replaced by a form of society in which employers, workmen and traders cooperated in ways which rendered armed force and nationality irrelevant. Later in the century Herbert Spencer distinguished between what he called 'militant' and 'industrial' social types. In his *Principles of Sociology* (1876–96) he said that in militant forms of society the whole people is nationally organised like an army with ranks, a chain of command and an imposed *esprit de corps*. For the latter to be possible the leadership has to combine political with religious and ceremonial functions. In such societies the industrial and commercial activities are subordinated to the requirements of the government, for which they constitute a 'permanent commissariat'.[2] In industrial types of society, on the other hand, cooperation is secured by voluntary means. 'Multitudinous objects', Spencer wrote, 'are achieved by spontaneously-evolved combinations of citizens governed representatively.'[3] In industrial types of society free exchange is the central economic feature, and freedom and the keeping of agreements are basic moral requirements. Thus the unity, hierarchy and use of force in the militant type of society are contrasted with the differentiation and freedom of the industrial type.

---

[1] *Œuvres de Saint-Simon et d'Enfantin* (Paris, 1865–76), Vol. 18. See Frank E. Manuel's *The New World of Henri Saint-Simon* (Harvard University Press, 1956), ch. 20.
[2] *Principles of Sociology* (3rd edn, London, 1885), Vol. 1, p. 549.
[3] *Ibid.*, p. 556.

Saint-Simon's view of 'industrial' society was largely based on J.-B. Say's account of the economic system, which in its turn was derived from Adam Smith's critique of mercantilism.[1] Spencer, for his part, was a liberal of the old school who watched with alarm as governments that called themselves liberal interfered more and more with economic affairs. The distinction between military and industrial[2] types of society was drawn, therefore, from an antisocialist, or at any rate an antimercantilist point of view. Furthermore, neither type exists without some admixture of the other, and existing societies are more or less military, more or less industrial. Indeed, from what we have said already in chapter I it is clear that if the 'industrial' type of society is to keep going there must be a government that enforces contracts and punishes fraud and violence, and hence some features of the military society are inevitable if anarchy is to be prevented. Since Spencer's day the movement towards collectivism which he saw and deplored has accelerated to such an extent that the sort of spontaneously regulated society he favoured seems very remote to us now.[3]

But these are not adequate reasons for neglecting the important truths that are expressed in the distinction between 'military' and 'industrial' or 'contractual' types of society. Advocates of state-provided welfare have generally considered themselves to be pacific and internationalist in their aims. But in spite of this the twentieth century has been a particularly warlike period. Collectivism, egalitarianism and neomercantilism, indeed, have been prominent features of a civilisation in which whole peoples have been slaughtered. The growth of science and technology has undoubtedly made this slaughter more efficient, but the coincidence of war and welfare state collectivism should make us think it possible that egalitarian collectivism and militarism are not as opposed to one another as is generally supposed.

[1] Manuel suggests that Saint-Simon was not sincere in writing this, as he says that 'in 1817 Saint-Simon posed as the popularizer of extreme *laissez-faire* liberalism . . .' (*The New World of Henri Saint-Simon*, p. 241).

[2] 'Industrial', in this usage, does not mean 'technological'. Perhaps 'commercial' or even 'contractual' would have been a more suitable designation.

[3] There are signs in some communist countries of a movement towards 'industrial' i.e. 'contractual' forms of organisation.

Should distributive justice overrule commutative justice?

Near the beginning of the present chapter it was argued that distributive justice requires a distributor. This is not a purely verbal point—indeed, the phrase 'distribution of wealth' does not itself imply that someone has distributed it. The point is this. A complex society that has developed through many vicissitudes of history is neither justly nor unjustly organised. When, however, people want it to be justly organised they imply that, since God has not done so, man must take it in hand and do what God has failed to do. As soon as people want society as a whole to be justly organised they imply that it should be brought under some unitary human control so that the government secures the just distribution that does not come about on its own. In a democratic society the voters are expected to elect a government to do this.

Now the question that needs to be considered is whether a state organised to move towards distributive justice can at the same time be organised to maintain commutative justice. Are these consistent aims or must they clash with one another? I suggest that there is a fundamental opposition. Commutative justice is found when freely made agreements are kept, and it is maintained when there are laws for punishing fraud and for enforcing the fulfilment of contracts. The state's prime functions are the prevention and repression of crimes and the maintenance of honest dealing. Humanity requires it to provide such help for the unfortunate as other agencies cannot ensure. But it is most unlikely that the ownership of wealth and incomes which results from this will coincide with what the political parties in a democratic electorate will consider just. In particular, collectivist parties consider that the just distribution of wealth and income would be a more equal distribution, and hence they use taxation as a means of equalising wealth and incomes as well as a means of paying for the enforcement of law and for helping the unfortunate.

Since taxation is not a voluntary payment, in democratic societies the better-off are forced to give up wealth in order to conform to the electorate's desire for distributive justice, and even if the distinctions of wealth are not very large, taxation is used to enforce the majority's view of what sort of distribution is proper. If someone is unwilling to contribute towards the cost of crime prevention, we feel he ought to be made to do so. If someone is unwilling to contribute towards the cost of helping those who are in dire want, we do not think it is wrong for taxation to be put upon him. But to be forced to make payments in order to secure a just distribution of wealth is a different matter, since there is no universal view on what such a distribution should be, and the individual is being forced to pay for something he may consider wrong. Furthermore, the larger the proportion of his income that is taken for purposes of public expenditure, the stronger the likelihood of inflation, and in consequence financial agreements of all kinds are interfered with because of the erosion in the value of money. Again, in the pursuit of distributive justice agreements between landowners and houseowners and between landlords and tenants are altered or abrogated. Trade unions, for one reason or another, are freed from the necessity to keep to their agreements, and bequests are diverted from the purposes intended by the donors. Thus the scope of coercion is widened and the possibilities for free agreements are diminished.

Trade unions were given their present privileged legal status at a time when their bargaining position was weak, and retain it at a time when it is very strong. It is now agreed by 'experts' whose convictions are formed under the influence of the trade union bureaucracy that it is impossible in this country to make changes in trade union law towards the sort of legal system that exists in other countries. The report of the *Royal Commission on Trade Unions and Employers' Associations 1965–1968* (Cmnd 3623) shows how difficult it is, to quote Andrew Shonfield's phrase (p. 288), to get consideration for 'the degree of regulation which should properly be applied to organisations wielding great authority in communities where the average citizen becomes progressively more vulnerable to what they do', in the face of an organisation defended by experts who can easily exploit the practical complications involved in the making of any change whatever.

It may be argued that it is quite right for commutative justice to give way before distributive justice, since the former is often based on a bargain imposed under unfair conditions in which the wealthy have all the advantages. We discussed the idea that buying and selling is unfair in capitalist societies when in chapter II we considered J. A. Hobson's account of the matter. We there concluded that Hobson unwittingly assumed that a fair bargain would be one carried out in the conditions of a competitive market. But the point that now needs to be made is that when distributive justice is placed above commutative justice, force is being advocated at the expense of voluntary agreement. Force, of course, is inseparable from government, and has to be used in order to prevent or punish murder, assault, fraud and theft. Everyone is against these crimes and everyone favours the force of government that is used to prevent them. But there is no such unanimity about what constitutes a failure in distributive justice in the community as a whole. I have suggested that the very conception of it assumes that there should be a distributor. Quite apart from that, the claims of desert, merit, achievement, effort and need complicate the issue to such an extent that egalitarians themselves have in recent years given up the attempt to assess their relative weightings. There are disagreements about what constitutes justice in a voluntary bargain, but they are capable of settlement and have been worked out over centuries in the law of commerce.

In practice, in democratic societies the answer to the question what constitutes a 'just' distribution of wealth varies as different groups and interests gain the ear of politicians. The prevailing interests try to get economists, sociologists and journalists to justify their policies, and are generally able to find some who are willing to do so. What a democratic collectivist government would most like to have would be a widespread belief that the principles behind its policies are morally necessary. In democratic societies this moral consensus is obtained, if at all, after much discussion and argument. But when a democratic government is deeply involved in economic affairs, there is a tendency for the discussion to take place within the terms of the immediate problems the government is facing. Criticism that calls the prevailing trends into question is apt to be regarded as irresponsible. Businessmen, academics and journalists are tempted to look at events within the context of governmental policy.

Since trade unions, professional organisations and industrial associations are constantly being asked to help in government, their leadership tends to get into the hands of men who are thought to be 'responsible' and 'constructive'. Businessmen are put in a difficult position, for if they refuse to cooperate in governmental plans they are accused of injuring the public interest, and if they do cooperate they are inevitably associated with the collectivism they may not agree with. In particular, as lines of production are costed by accountants employed by the government, the notion of a 'fair' or 'reasonable' profit gets accepted. But this, as I argued in chapter II, is, in effect, to abandon the conception of profit altogether and to assimilate it to a fee or to a salary—at any rate to something that can be contracted for. I do not think that this particular aspect of governmental planning has been sufficiently noticed. Once a certain rate of profit is regarded as 'reasonable' or 'fair', profit is no longer playing the part it used to play in economic affairs, and the retention of the word only serves to disguise the essential change that the economic system is undergoing. Sometimes 'fair' profits are profits which monopolists in collusion with governments hope to obtain as a result of their collusion.

However that may be, it is clear that democratic collectivist governments, concerned as they are with distributive justice, concerned, that is, with distribution by the government in terms of a moral rule, are bound to want this rule to be accepted by everyone. Now there is a moral principle which all civilised peoples accept, the so-called Golden Rule, according to which people should treat others as they would wish others to treat them. What this principle enunciates is the idea that no one should expect others to treat him as a unique and special case, as entitled to more consideration than others just because he is the individual he in fact is. As regards commutative justice this means that no one is entitled to argue that, whereas others must keep their engagements to him, he is under no obligation to keep his engagements to them. Certainly if someone were to argue in this way, or were to act as though he had taken up this point of view, he would be going against a central feature of civilised morality.

But does the Golden Rule apply to distributive justice as well? Egalitarian collectivists appear to suppose that it does, in that they argue that it is a violation of distributive justice for an individual to be discriminated against, that is, for him not to get the same treatment as others when there is no difference in his situation that requires this. Someone, for example, goes into a nursing home for private medical treatment, whereas someone else who cannot or will not afford it (i.e. prefers to spend his money on motoring or something else) waits much longer and goes into a hospital where he cannot get the privacy he would like. Egalitarians would regard this as a violation of distributive justice if both people were in need of private treatment for, it is supposed, in these circumstances there is discrimination in favour of the man who pays, and two individuals whose needs are similar receive unequal treatment just because one is willing to pay and the other will not or cannot.

But we must ask who does the discriminating here. There would be unjust discrimination[1] if those responsible for allocating beds under some national health scheme gave more favourable conditions to one than to another who equally needed them when it was possible to give similar conditions to both. But when there is freedom to pay for the conditions that some people want, no one discriminates when one person has less favourable conditions than another whose plight is the same as his. To talk as though there is unjust discrimination in such circumstances is *to assume* that all medical care *ought to be* under a single public control, and such an assumption will only be made when a large part of it already is. To attack 'discrimination', therefore, rather than callousness or poverty, is really to call for a single state system. Now while it is true that the Golden Rule prohibits selfishness, fraud and lack of consideration for others, it can hardly be taken to imply that there should be no private medicine, housing or education.

Someone whose duty it is to administer a rule must do so justly, that is, he must follow the rule in such a way as not to favour some by comparison with others. He is required to treat equal cases equally, and if one party is treated differently from another there must be some relevant ground for this. But it does not follow from this rule of distributive justice that *no*

---

[1] It is significant of the trend towards an unthinking egalitarianism that the word 'discrimination', which in aesthetic contexts is regarded as essential and desirable, is, in moral contexts, taken in a pejorative sense, so that 'unjust discrimination' tends to become pleonastic. Similarly 'segregation' is taken to mean 'undesirable segregation' and 'selection' to mean 'undesirable selection'.

one should treat one person differently from another without some reason for doing so. If it did, then friendship would be impossible, since friends do not generally have reasons for being friends. People have reasons for being allies or business partners or political associates, but it is possible to have friends who are none of these, and hence to have friends for no reasons whatsoever. The existence of friendship, therefore, is a proof that the Golden Rule does not imply that distributive justice should prevail in all human relationships.[1] If what I have said is right, then distributive justice is applicable only where there is an authority applying a rule of distribution. To press for universal distributive justice, therefore, is to press for a universal authority.[2] It is generally admitted that totalitarian socialism requires such an authority, but it is now clear that democratic socialism requires one too. Forced fraternity or compulsory integration is an essential characteristic of egalitarian collectivist society.

We have now seen what truth there is in Spencer's idea that socialist societies are types of 'militant' society. In socialist societies the governments hope for a much wider range of moral agreement than obtains in non-socialist societies, and endeavour to obtain it, not only by argument and persuasion, but also by prohibiting behaviour which many members of the community regard as right or permissible. Thus in socialist societies the political leaders endeavour to secure a moral authority for their aims, and although moral authority is different from ecclesiastical authority it is the nearest approach to it that a secular society can offer. For it involves at least the suggestion and frequently the assertion that opponents of the government are wicked men. When governments claim to speak with moral authority on topics that permit of genuine moral disagreement they act as a sort of secular church fulminating

[1] Cf. Dr Aurel Kolnai's paper, 'The Moral Theme in Political Division', *Philosophy*, 1960, pp. 214–54, especially p. 254: 'The basic moral intuitions of mankind—which Right and Left alike cannot but take for granted as a premise for their respective moral appeal—provide no solution, except in a prohibitive and limiting sense, for the permanent or topical problems of political organisation and choice.'
[2] Cf. P. Dognin's 'Échange et "justice" commutative selon K. Marx', in *Archives de Philosophic de Droit* (No. 12): *Marx et le Droit Moderne* (Paris, 1967). Professor Dognin quotes from Proudhon: 'The family is the sphere of authority and subordination; and if communism is to be logical, it will recognize that in taking the family as the type of society, it ends in despotism' (p. 32). Perhaps there is less despotism in families now because it is being transferred to the state.

against heretics. In the end, however, the heretics against democratic socialism are not likely to be burned, but smothered rather by the weight of officially generated opinion.

The resulting form of society need not be hierarchical but it must be bureaucratic.[1] Professor Hayek has pointed out[2] that a centrally organised economic plan can no more be drawn up or executed by democratic discussion of details than an army can carry out a campaign by democratic procedures. Bureaucrats are needed, not merely because they are experts—frequently they are not—but because men are needed to take decisions as events unfold, and neither legislators nor elected ministers are often in a position to intervene. Nationalised industries, government departments and state welfare organisations all have to be organised in bureaucratic forms with controlling directors and committees and chains of command and responsibility. Recruitment into them may be by merit and hence they may offer a career to talent. But when there are more of such bodies and they increase in numbers, as necessarily happens with the move towards collectivism, fundamental changes take place in the society as a whole. Democratic control and independent criticism must be made more difficult. When a large part of the information about economic statistics or administrative arrangements is collected and issued by the government, investigators and critics are forced to approach the very officials they may criticise for the information that might give substance to their criticisms. The officials will generally defend themselves, their superiors and the system in which they hold positions of responsibility. 'Cooperative' and 'public-spirited' enquirers will be favoured. Writers who hope for these favours will insensibly find themselves supporting a 'public interest' that the government itself has defined. Even in the merely partial collectivism under which we now live, consultative committees, parents' associations and other such bodies are treated with a somewhat contemptuous toleration. But as collectivism is further extended, these bodies become agencies for explaining and justifying the government's decisions, as the trade unions have become in the 'people's democracies'. There

---

[1] In the 'redeployment' of labour executed by the government in 1966–67, by far the largest number went into governmental agencies.
[2] *The Road to Serfdom* (Routledge, 1944), ch. V.

are the beginnings of such developments in the society we live in, but if they are recognised they can be dealt with. If on the other hand, they are not recognised, a social order will grow up from which independent thought and action have been unwittingly excluded.

V. Some Reflections on Planning and Predicting

Is a centrally planned economy inevitable?

So far I have endeavoured to do two things. First, I have criticised the arguments and assumptions of those who oppose systems of free market enterprise on moral grounds. Second, I have argued that the egalitarian collectivist alternative to a system of competitive markets is bound to lead to the authoritarian imposition of a state-controlled morality. In my discussion so far I have assumed that a system in which consumers, individual entrepreneurs and firms compete in their various ways is possible, and that potentially maleficent monopolies can be somehow got rid of. But in his Reith Lectures delivered in 1966 and in *The New Industrial State* (Hamish Hamilton, 1967) Professor J. K. Galbraith has argued that the growth of large-scale technology has made competitive markets obsolete.[1]

Galbraith asserts that in consequence of the types of technology now in use, even very large firms cannot take risks in employing the large amounts of capital needed for the development of their products. They therefore ensure that their product is bought by preparing the way for it with advertisement, and they see to it that there is no competition in settling the price. In effect, according to Galbraith, they make the consumers want what the producers wish to sell, and they determine the price so as to cover their outlays and to provide capital for future developments. But they can only do this if the consumers they 'manage' (Galbraith's word) have the money to pay the prices; and to see to it that they have, the government is encouraged to step in to maintain total demand by monetary management, to limit wage demands, to provide the training needed in the technological industries (hence the growth of higher education in recent years), and to undertake the very

---

[1] He says that in the United States 'faith in free enterprise is one of the minor branches of theology' (*The Listener*, 17 Nov., 1966, p. 711). Galbraith, of course, expects his readers to conclude that it is therefore quite ridiculous.

great risks involved in such new industries as those concerned with atomic power and space travel.[1] 'We may assume', he says, 'that there has been an interaction between state and firm which has brought the two to a unity of view.'[2]

According to Galbraith modern industrial planning is autonomous in the sense that it is a primary agency that makes other practices and institutions follow in its wake. Hence the modern style of industrial production puts the old style of industrial entrepreneur out of business, yet at the same time it makes it impossible for democratic politicians to control it. For the decisions of large-scale industry are, 'if it is to be efficient, somewhat authoritarian'.[3] He concludes that the differences between what is falsely called 'free enterprise' in the United States and the socialist societies of Eastern Europe have been much exaggerated, and that there is little that individuals can do to alter the technological autonomy which leads to their convergence. What individuals can try to do is to set up aesthetic objectives which are not engendered within the industrial organisation itself. But if individuals oppose the state they will only be helping the industrial organisation to extend its control for, according to Galbraith, industrial organisation is so powerful that it is only through the state that it can in any way be limited. 'It is through the state', he writes, 'that the society must assert the superior claims of aesthetic over economic goals, and particularly of environment over cost.'[4] If Galbraith is right, then, the inevitable future is a society under the 'somewhat authoritarian' control of industrial managers who may be persuaded by the state to pay some attention to the beauties of the human and natural environment as they manage consumers, fix prices and expand their operations.

This view of Galbraith's is an elaborately modulated outcry of helpless disillusion rather than an analysis of our present social situation, but even so it calls for a number of comments. Galbraith argues as if what a determined advertising campaign may achieve for an individual detergent manufacturer can

---

[1] *The Listener*, 8 Dec. 1966, pp. 841–42.
[2] *Ibid.*, p. 853.
[3] 'The technical complexity and planning and associated scale of operations that took power from the capitalist entrepreneur and lodged it in the body of the firm, removed it from the reach of social control' (*The Listener*, 15 Dec. 1966, p. 882).
[4] *The Listener*, 22 Dec. 1966, p. 918.

be achieved for the whole of industry, but the near-collapse, to take one example, of the shipbuilding industry in this country is evidence to the contrary. The successes of advertising take place when a demand exists that can be evoked, extended or transferred from one product to another, but to create demand or even to manage it is a very different proposition. I endeavoured to show in chapter II that markets are not independent of the society in which they function, but presuppose all sorts of other activities. In societies where many different activities flourish, this variety will be reflected in the many different things that people want. Wants can be managed by industrialists and by governments only in societies where there are few centres of independent activity. In effect, Galbraith is arguing that in our own day technological and industrial management is the sole source of independent ('autonomous') activity. He is implying that men's wants are so limited and so feeble that a fairly small group of scientists, technologists and business administrators can control them. In his view of our society the only possible counterbalance to large-scale industry is the desire to enjoy beauty, while religion, intellectual self-development, the concern for justice and for freedom, and the striving for moral integrity are assumed to be ineffective.

Galbraith is so far correct in that the very intellectual development which encouraged the growth of modern science and its technological applications has discouraged religious beliefs and has weakened religious institutions. Furthermore the cult of youth and of contemporaneity tends to attribute merit to what is new and to lessen concern for monuments of the past, whether in landscape, buildings or literature. (Conservationists are apt to be of a conservative frame of mind.) Traditional morality, too, tends to be regarded as outmoded. It is possible however, to recognise that this is widely believed without going to the extreme of holding that the wish for aesthetic enjoyment is the only curb on complete technological control over society. If this were so, then the case would indeed be bad, since aesthetic taste is variable and very easily modified. But I suggest that there are many people with a concern for freedom and spontaneity whose wants are not manufactured by the large industrial concerns. To ask them, as Galbraith does, to put their trust in state intervention on their behalf is to acquiesce in the existing or emerging *status quo*. It has been said[1] that Galbraith's views may have released powerful and radical forces, but surely what they suggest is that there is practically nothing that can be done to alter the present trends, and that therefore the ruling authorities have to be submitted to in the hope that they will not destroy too much beauty. Whether Galbraith thinks that nothing else is worth preserving or that everything else has already gone without possibility of return he does not say.

It is interesting to notice that in *The New Industrial State* Professor Galbraith considers that universities have a part to play in influencing governments to allow scope for cultural (which for Galbraith seems to mean aesthetic) activities.[2] This might be useful, although not all university planning experts put beauty before industrial growth, and professors of Fine Art may not be listened to. Indeed, universities might be torn apart if one expert is paid to testify on one side and another on the opposite, even if by this means sweetness and light are brought to the tribunal proceedings. But universities are now being invaded by the idea that markets are essentially wicked and that demand is created and corrupted by irresponsible business corporations. Professor Herbert Marcuse, the rich man's Galbraith, puts forward Galbraithian ideas in sub-Galbraithian prose, writing of 'free competition at administered prices, a free press that censors itself, free choice between brands and gadgets'.[3] Marcuse's admirers in the universities seek to destroy the organisations that Galbraith thinks we must submit to and might influence, and they think that universities themselves are creatures of the corrupting bodies. What can a follower of Galbraith say in the face of all this?

---

[1] *The Times Business News*, 4 Sept. 1967, p. 21, referring to *The New Industrial State*: 'If the ideas of this book do gain wide acceptance, the professor may turn out to have loosed far more powerful and radical forces than his own gently chaffing tone suggests. For his critique is at least as ambitious in scope, as appealing in its simplicity and as alarming in its implication as Marx's ever was.'

[2] Cf. Raymond Ruyer, *Éloge de la Société de Consommation* (Paris, 1969): 'The remedy proposed by Galbraith: development of countervailing powers: universities, scientific research, astronautics, consists in adding to the military plans cultural plans, financed by the tax-payers. These will be less monstrous but in the end perhaps just as mortal, as is shown today by the enormous expenditure on universities and the instruction at great expense of an intellectual proletariat. Galbraith wants to cure the plague by inoculating the patient with cholera' (pp. 119–20).

[3] *One-dimensional Man* (Routledge, 1964), paperback edition, 1968, p. 23.

Professor Galbraith's views on the organisation and economic power of large industrial concerns have been criticised in some detail by Professor G. C. Allen[1] who points out that giant concerns meet with troubles, fluctuations and even disasters, and gives evidence to show that it is false to suppose that there is 'a steady progression from highly competitive markets to monopoly'.[2] He points out that large firms compete with one another, and although they do sometimes create demand (small firms do this too), they do not manage and control it to the extent that Galbraith's argument requires. Those who have studied British industry have not found it dominated by monopoly, and the monopoly of the nationalised Coal Board has not been able to prevent the demand for competing fuels. 'In 1950', Allen writes, 'the National Coal Board enjoyed the virtual monopoly of fuel supplies in this country. Today it is one of several powerful competitors for the fuel and power market.'[3]

Galbraith has no regrets for the competitive markets which he says have now ceased to have importance, and yet he seems to view with distaste the inevitable subjection to large firms in league with government which he says have replaced it. Perhaps he would have preferred democratic socialism, but since he thinks this is now impracticable, his only hope is that the democratic remnant will influence the state to provide oases of beauty in a world of machines, bureaucracies and standardised mass amusements. By adopting a collectivist attitude towards industrial authoritarianism, Galbraith and his followers make it clear that they intend merely to sit back and take what comes. But if Galbraith is wrong in his diagnosis, there are good prospects for opposition to monopolies of all kinds and opposition to attempts by governments to plan economic circumstances from the centre. If industrial monopoly under the aegis of the state is not inevitable, then there is much to be gained by criticising the collectivism that fosters its formation. Galbraith is not likely to release powerful and radical forces, but is rather a prophet of the bandwagon disguised as Solomon Eagle.[4]

---

[1] *Economic Fact and Fantasy. A Rejoinder to Galbraith's Reith Lectures.* Institute of Economic Affairs, Occasional Paper 14, 1967.

[2] *Ibid.*, p. 21.   [3] *Economic Fact and Fantasy*, p. 29.

[4] According to Daniel Defoe in *A Journal of the Plague Year*, Solomon Eagle was an 'enthusiast' who during the Plague of London 'went about denouncing judgment upon the city in a frightful manner'. 'What he said, or pretended, indeed I could not learn,' said Defoe, and Galbraith's intentions are similarly obscure.

Centralised planning and technological advance

We have seen that according to Galbraith modern industrial and technological planning is 'autonomous'. There is no need to accept the whole of his view to recognise that the development of natural science and technology is an extremely powerful element in contemporary society. The researches of Lord Rutherford, for example, led to the atomic bomb and to atomic fuel, to destruction, constant menace, new military strategies, new methods of curing diseases and new forms of motive power. Rutherford's discoveries were developed by technologists under the stress of war, and present soldiers, politicians and ordinary citizens with new dangers and new hopes. New materials, new machines, new methods of prolonging life constantly affect human relationships.

Some of the social effects of new discoveries can be foreseen, but it is unlikely that they all can be. Will the widespread use of contraceptive pills in advanced countries, for example, stabilise the population there or will it lead to a reduction? No one knows. No one knows, furthermore, what new discoveries and inventions will be made. Industrial firms, of course, have research workers trying to solve particular problems, and governments develop particular types of weapon in response to what they believe other governments are doing, and hence reasonable forecasts can be made about the probable results of these researches. But discoveries are sometimes made by accident, or as byproducts of a line of enquiry with quite other objectives. Sometimes discoveries involve quite a new way of looking at things, as when the concept of inertia was conceived, or as when light was conceived in terms of waves instead of in terms of corpuscles. The trouble with accidents, byproducts and new conceptions is not that they are *difficult* to predict, but that it is and must be *impossible* to predict them. For in predicting accidents, byproducts and new conceptions the predictor would already have made the discovery or formed the new conception and would not be predicting.[1]

[1] I made this point in 'Comte's Positivism and the science of society', *Philosophy* 1951, where references are given. Sir Karl Popper in the Preface to *The Poverty of Historicism* (Routledge, 1957) gives another argument (first formulated by him in 1950) to show that 'we cannot predict, by rational or scientific methods, the future growth of our scientific knowledge' (pp. ix–x). F. H. Bradley had argued to a similar conclusion in his *The Presuppositions of Critical History* (Oxford University Press, 1875). Carlyle, in an early essay, stated the point without argument.

We have seen that scientific and technological discoveries have considerable effects on the development of society. It follows that societies in which scientific and technological discovery is particularly frequent must be societies in which predictions of their future condition is particularly hazardous. Our society is certainly such a society, and hence all predictions of its future must be tentative.

Certain qualifications now need to be made. A scientific discovery may not have social repercussions for some considerable time after it has been made, and may not, indeed, have any such effects at all. Again, once a scientific discovery has been made, some of its technological and social effects may be foreseen and provided for. Furthermore, a technologically educated government (or firm) may foresee certain effects of a new invention and take steps to prevent it from being developed. Like 'Breakages Limited' in Shaw's play, it may even suppress a new invention or postpone its use. Nevertheless, the general effect of rapid scientific and technological advance is rapid social change and a failure to foresee what form it will take. The more rapid and widespread the technological advances are the more likely it is that social changes will occur that no one has anticipated.

But 'planners' of all parties urge *both* that rapid technological advance is desirable, *and* that the economy should be brought under centralised control. But any technological advance, whether by private firms or governments is bound to make control of the economy more difficult, and to defeat, from time to time, the schemes of the planners. The planners could try to keep the time-gap between scientific discovery and technological application as wide as possible. They could try to keep new inventions in cold storage until their implementation was opportune. They could withdraw funds from research or switch them from one area of investigation to another. But the range of scientific discovery and technological invention is enormous, and as specialisation increases, it becomes more difficult for any man or even committee to know what is afoot everywhere. Even if planning of the whole economy were a valid concept (in fact it is a confused one), and even if it were a feasible economic exercise (and this may well be doubted), the planners would still be faced with the paradox that the more successfully science and technology are pursued the more uncontrollable they become and the more social surprises they will give rise to. Scientists and technologists necessarily make the central planner's task impossible.

In an article in *The Economist*[1] entitled 'A Superior Snakes and Ladders' reference is made to a conference[2] at Strath-clyde University attended by market researchers, economists, systems analysts, mathematicians, logicians, sociologists, pure and applied scientists and businessmen. The object of the conference was to consider how scientific advances and tech-nological inventions and the resulting social repercussions and changes in demand could be predicted. The author confirms my doubts expressed above, that discoveries that involve looking at established facts in a new way are particularly hard —I would say impossible—to predict, but he seems to think that, because scientific research is now so well organised, even such discoveries might be predicted with some fairly high degree of probability. He recognises, however, that the prob-lem of predicting *when* a new technological discovery will be made is extremely difficult, and that forecasts of demand based on the so-called 'Delphi' technique of collecting the opinions of large numbers of experts are bound to be risky. After going on to note the difficulties that arise in integrating the evidence of mathematicians, technologists, economists, etc., he con-cludes: 'The magnitude of the problems can be gauged from our continuing inability to produce a workable and up-to-date input–output table of the economy, despite all the statistics. Without one, any closely engineered national plan will break down—just as the first one did.' This seems to call for the following comments.

(*a*) Accidents and new ways of regarding the facts *cannot, logically* cannot, be predicted. To attempt to do so is merely to attempt to hasten up scientific and technological advance by shock methods.

(*b*) It is true that those in the know can sometimes foresee various *types* of scientific or technological discovery that are, so to say, already in the pipeline. Even then, as the writer in

[1] 6 July 1968.
[2] Papers read at the conference and published in *Technological Forecasting*, (ed. R. V. Arnfield), Edinburgh University Press, 1969.

The Economist points out, timing is very important, since the course of events may be very different if the order of two discoveries or inventions is different. In any case, these limited predictions can be made only if it is assumed that no very fundamental discovery will make them irrelevant.

(*c*) Once it is admitted that predictions of further discoveries and inventions only allow of probability, it has also to be admitted that their practical utility must be limited, and it always remains possible that plans based on them will turn out disastrously.

(*d*) If we could be quite sure that no other unforeseen occurrences would interfere with our social plans, we could make them with confidence. Those who want to plan human society on a very large scale are therefore tempted to try to keep large parts of society as stable as they can. As their plan progresses they will get more and more irritated at anyone who plays the joker. They can only stop him by preventing him from playing at all. There can be no important place in such a society for spontaneous behaviour. Social prediction on a large scale is easiest in repetitive or traditional and hardest in progressive forms of society. Those who want to predict and make sure cannot allow private initiatives. They are driven towards totalitarianism.

The events in France during May and June 1968 are very instructive in this context. The French 'planners' had devised what *dirigistes* elsewhere have commended as a well-organised and successful set of financial, economic and industrial measures which secured a strong franc and an apparent unity. The completely unexpected students' revolution and the confused reactions to it brought about a situation which no one had foreseen. Within a few days the whole economic outlook was transformed in ways which the planners had not wanted.

(*e*) A further difficulty in the way of long-term planning for the future is that it seems likely that future generations will want different things from what we want, or, to put it pompously, will have different systems of values from ours. If this is so, to plan for the sort of thing that the present generation wants would be to produce a gigantic white elephant that future generations would not know what to do with. 'Futurologists', therefore, as those who study how to plan and foresee the future call themselves, find it necessary to consider how people are likely to evaluate the choices open to them in the year 1985[1] or the year 2000.[2] A large number of learned articles have been written on this subject, and in 1967 a journal called *The Futurist* was founded in the USA by the World Future Society. A contributor to this journal suggests that in the future such literary themes as adversity, death and sexual frustration will mean little 'in a world of affluence, near-immortality and instant sex'.

Attempts are made at a serious assessment of this problem in *Values and the Future*.[3] One of the contributors, after commenting on the rapid social and hence 'value change' in our own generation, looks forward to the institution of a new profession of 'value impact forecasters'. Professor Rescher gives some analysis of what can be meant by 'value change', suggesting that it can mean a growth or diminution of the adherents of a specific value, a greater or less commitment to it by its adherents, extension or diminution of the range of its application, and so on. He thinks that personal independence may be less valued in the future ('we may consider the Southern California of today as setting the pattern for the America of the future'[4]), that 'intelligence and inventiveness' will 'probably be in the ascendant for many years ahead', that 'gadgetry' will increase, that nationalism will diminish, that family links will loosen. Professor Galbraith contributes to this volume, and he predicts that the power of trade unions will decline as the numbers of production workers are reduced, and that the 'educational estate', instead of being subordinated to the business community, will be needed to give it leadership and advice. 'The pre-Cambrian entrepreneur who once denounced long-haired and radical professors has been warned about hurting the recruitment programme.' It is interesting to compare this with the view of Ruyer quoted on p. 89 above.

In an excellent article, 'Futurology and the problem of values' (*International Social Science Journal*, Vol. 21, no. 4, 1969, an issue devoted to futurology) Dr Irene Taviss raises some

[1] The Horizen 1985 Commission in France.
[2] H. Kahn and A. J. Wiener, *The Year 2000* (Collier-Macmillan, 1967).
[3] Kurt Baier and Nicholas Rescher, eds., *Values and the Future*, New York, Free Press, 1969.
[4] Written before the burning down of the Bank of America at Santa Barbara on 28 February 1970.

sceptical questions. Are not futurologists really commenting on their own times rather than predicting what will come? (One could compare 'instant sex' with the dreams of Ben Jonson's Sir Epicure Mammon.) Are they not unduly optimistic, along the lines of the Liberal Establishment? What are the reasons for supposing that in some cases (e.g. democracy) threats to a value will upgrade it in the future and in other cases (e.g. privacy) threats are likely to downgrade it? Who should do the value forecasting? And as the forecasts will inevitably be linked with normative *plans*, should the planning be done by experts, by a plurality of agencies, or by advocates of some particular plan?

The merging of prediction into planning and control is, of course, the most serious aspect of what might otherwise be regarded as a sort of academic *Old Moore's Almanac*. In this same volume an article entitled 'Imagination and the future' by Dr Robert Jungk, founder of the Institut für Zukunftsfragen in Vienna, shows how futurology and centralised planning can be regarded as a sort of romantic 'social titanism', to use a phrase at one time used in Russia. Of man aware of the ubiquity of change Dr Jungk writes:

Instead of the firmly circumscribed, the everchanging would be recognised as the condition of his existence. But this would mean a readjustment of man's inner being, which would probably have to go even deeper than the Copernican system, as it would require the abandonment of all firm certainties and the recognition of perpetual change. In such a 'floating world' creative imagination will then become man's prime faculty . . . for he will be logically forecasting the future, no longer on the basis of supposedly eternal laws, but conjuring it forth from within himself (p. 562).

The planning prophet regards himself as producing future generations as if they were verses in a poem of his own making. Planning becomes the realisation of kaleidoscopic dreams.

VI. Summary and Conclusions

Collectivists of various sorts have said that the pursuit of profit by businessmen and firms spreads greed throughout the community. We have argued that economic activities are only a part of what is done in civilised societies. The making of profits need not be the sole concern of those who engage in business, and is sometimes a means of obtaining the wherewithal for enterprises of non-pecuniary and philanthropic importance. Not all the evils in capitalist societies are due to profit-seeking and profit-making. They may be due to a failure in moral education, to deficiencies in public spirit and *individual* morality rather than to the ways in which economic activities are organised. Competitive markets influence the rest of society, but they are themselves affected by moral, religious and aesthetic considerations. It is begging the question to say that the evils of societies in which business is carried on competitively for profit are wholly or mainly due to their economic arrangements. It may well be, as Hayek suggests, that under a competitive system bad men can do least harm.

Those taking part in competitive markets are not consciously devoting themselves to the common weal, nor are they engaged in acts of individual charity. Devotion, friendship, self-sacrifice are found in other circumstances of man's life, in their personal relationships and family concerns. In exchanging goods and services we may hope for honesty and diligence and perhaps forbearance but, just as the players in a game try to win and expect their opponents to play to win also, so in competitive markets the participants, from large producing firms to individual purchasers, are trying to do as well for themselves as possible.

Carlyle, Ruskin and Tawney considered that businessmen are inferior to such professional men as doctors, lawyers and soldiers, because the latter, they held, put service before profit, and would sacrifice their lives if need be, and were in honour bound to do their very best work. I have suggested that such moral differences as there are between businessmen and professional men are due to the differences in their work and circumstances. An important difference is that the businessman finances his productions and gains a profit or incurs a loss at the end of this operation, whereas many professional men work for fees or salaries. Hence the latter contract with their clients or employer for what they receive, whereas the businessman's profit is not something for which he has any contractual entitlement. To call for the assimilation of profits to professional fees or salaries is, therefore, to call for the abolition of the competitive market system. This connection is not generally noticed by those who are impressed by Ruskin's and Tawney's rhetoric.

J. A. Hobson was discussed as representative of those who regard trading as wicked in that it requires individuals and firms to threaten rivals or employees with starvation, and is hence fundamentally coercive. I suggested that in competitive markets coercion is at a minimum and that bargaining with threats is more characteristic of political behaviour. When employees are organised in trade unions the threats often come from them. The moral condemnation of employers that is widespread today is based on arguments which were not overwhelmingly strong when first put forward and are irrelevant in present circumstances.

Collectivists believe that competition is a state of strife, discord, antagonism and unseemly rivalry, and hence that it is morally noxious. But it is necessary to distinguish different types of competition. Competition for a prize, for example, need not be striving *against* one another, but only *for* the prize. Competitors in industry and commerce are frequently in this non-antagonistic relation towards one another. There is also *impersonal* competition, in which individual animals, species, firms and whole industries are injured or eliminated if they fail to adapt to changing circumstances. The phrase 'law of the jungle' (or, more recently, 'free-for-all') is not always apt even when applied to biological competition, and is less so when applied to firms and industries. The growth of trade unions and of similar protective and aggressive organisations has led to some replacement of non-antagonistic peaceful competition by deliberate manœuvring for getting and increasing power. What the newspapers call 'show-downs' between unions and employers' associations result from a breakdown of economic competition and should not be regarded as outcomes or exercises of it. I have suggested that competition, and perhaps rivalry and antagonism between ultimate consumers, is intensified by the spread of the attitude that opposes saving and encourages unlimited consumption. 'The right to be happy' has as its consequence the possibility of struggling to 'keep up with the Joneses'.

At this point we may call attention to a further important consequence of the present forms of trade union organisation in Great Britain. The unions bargain with the employers for a wage that is the same for all members of each category of workmen. This may be added to by overtime (often restricted by the union) or by output bonuses (which, again, are generally limited), but by and large individuals are not allowed to obtain benefits for themselves as a result of individual agreements. The policy of 'one out, all out' leads to the conclusion 'one up, all up'. In consequence, few individuals see any prospect of improving their financial position by means of special *individual* skill or industry, and any incentive to exercise it is therefore diminished if not completely destroyed. Payment in terms reached by bargains that concern only categories of workers depresses individual achievement and personal ambition. Furthermore, it gives rise to a dimly felt hopelessness as individuals are merged in a group controlled by men whose ambition is for power rather than for money. The very men who lead the collective activities of their workmates might, in different circumstances, use their energies and abilities in work that would benefit both themselves and the concern they work for. Perhaps they take on such leadership because they see no other means of utilising their powers or of distinguishing themselves from the mass. Few professional people realise the individual hopelessness on which collective trade union 'militancy' depends. Both the militant leader and his passive followers are in the toils of a system which continuously depresses the hopes that might stimulate individual excellence.[1]

[1] Incidentally, it would be interesting to estimate the *costs* of industrial bargaining apart from losses due to strikes. What is the cost of the whole trade union organisation and the elements within employing bodies that exist to bargain with the unions? The bill would also include the costs of the relevant parts of the Department of Employment and Productivity and of the officials and lawyers which the Royal Commission on Trade Unions and Employers' Associations think necessary for the future working of industrial relations.

There are some things, such as honour or criminal services, which ought never to be bought and sold, but education, medical care and housing are not among them. When certain basic needs are provided for in proportion to need by governments out of taxation, there must follow a tendency for individuals to attribute more importance to luxury spending than they would or could do if they had to provide for these basic needs out of their own disposable incomes. If the government forces its priorities on everyone, then the priorities of each individual in the disposal of his remaining income are priorities within a less essential range. What began as a humanitarian campaign to help the unfortunate could end as a system of bureaucratic control over a population of irresponsible and endlessly dissatisfied seekers after gratification.[1]

The form of collectivism most favoured in Britain aims to get basic welfare (education, medical care and perhaps housing) distributed in accordance with need rather than by purchase in competitive markets. The complex bureaucracies necessary to carry this out, however, along with their academic and journalistic supporters, would make independent discussion of the social and moral implications increasingly unlikely and practically ineffective. Once, indeed, they are established in their full panoply radical criticism is regarded as 'unrealistic'. Furthermore, in developed societies as many people as possible should have the opportunity of personal choice in these items of welfare, as well as in food, apparel and amusement. Welfare planners wish to force everyone to integrate, but in such a community of forced friends there would still be competition, both to obtain a maximum of the services provided and to obtain special benefits. Plausible pleaders, political lobbyists and sea-lawyers might set the tone.

In so far as egalitarian collectivists wish to secure distributive justice throughout society they must require the establishment of a distributor of justice who will from time to time (or even continually if there is inflation) override commutative justice. Even democratic collectivism, therefore,

[1] The following passage, headed 'The "conspiracy of dishonesty" on psychiatry' appeared in the *Glasgow Herald*, 29 April 1967: 'Dr Forrest quotes Professor Galbraith as suggesting that when customers have satisfied their more pressing needs for cars, washing machines and refrigerators, they tend to wish to purchase happiness, and turn to the psychiatrist as the most appropriate vendor.' Dr Forrest is Consultant Psychiatrist at the Royal Edinburgh Hospital.

tends to become authoritarian. By claiming moral authority for their schemes democratic socialists come to regard those who oppose them as a sort of moral heretic who must ultimately be treated as criminals if they refuse to admit their errors. In a letter to *The Times*, 5 Sept. 1967, R. G. Wallace, General Secretary of the Socialist Educational Association, writing about the Appeal Court's decision on the Enfield comprehensive schools, ends his letter as follows: 'We are told that we live in an age of consensus politics. The new Secretary of State may feel that the present law makes the national consensus in favour of comprehensive education difficult to achieve and that the time has come to change the law.' What this means is that the law should be changed so as to *bring about* or *enforce* a consensus. No doubt what Mr Wallace intended it to mean is that there is already a consensus in favour of comprehensive education and that therefore it should be enforced upon those few who do not want it. A few months before this letter was written the parties in local government who supported comprehensive education had suffered a severe setback at the polls. What it is most important to notice, however, is that 'consensus' is the mid-twentieth-century euphemism for 'orthodoxy'. Antisocialists, too, sometimes seek 'consensus', but should beware lest they find themselves committed to the enforcement of a moral and social orthodoxy.

'Galbraithism' is an elaborate expression of confused despair, not a realistic policy.

Since a comprehensive and rapidly developing technology involves constant movement into the unpredictable, centralised economic planning will always meet with disappointment in societies in which science and technology play a major role. In addition, then, to the many economic objections to a centrally planned economy, there is the further objection that a rapidly advancing technology makes it impossible to obtain the data essential for a centralised economic plan. Competitive markets are likely to do less harm than centralised economic planning and to give more scope for intellectual and moral excellence. A centrally planned economy is bound to monopolise ideas and even to ration them, whereas in a society where competitive markets prevail it is not only trade, but also thoughts and men that are free.

Index